DECODING THE TORAH

RABBI KIRT A. SCHNEIDER

Decoding the Torah by Rabbi Kirt A. Schneider
Published by Charisma House, an imprint of Charisma Media
1150 Greenwood Blvd., Lake Mary, Florida 32746

For more resources like this, visit MyCharismaShop.com and the author's website at DiscoveringtheJewishJesus.com.

Cataloging-in-Publication Data is on file with the Library of Congress.
International Standard Book Number: 978-1-63641-413-3
E-book ISBN: 978-1-63641-414-0

1 2024
Printed in the United States of America

CONTENTS

SPECIAL THANKS

It is very important to me to express my sincere appreciation to my developmental editor, Adrienne Gaines, with Charisma Media, for her patience, support, and invaluable professional feedback.

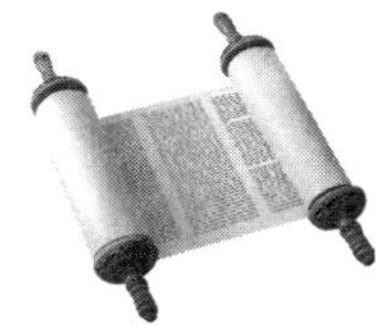

INTRODUCTION

NOT LONG AFTER I became a believer in Jesus, I sought to understand how I as a Jew could walk out my faith in Yeshua (Jesus) without losing my Jewish identity. I knew unequivocally that as followers of Messiah we are not under the Law, but I wanted to know, "How does the Law given to Moses and the Israelites apply to me? Which of the commandments am I to keep?"

I asked other Jewish believers in Messiah Jesus this question and was advised to keep Shabbat (the Sabbath), eat kosher, and wear tzitzit (the fringes you see on the four corners of a Jewish prayer shawl), but their recommendations stopped there. Something in me was not content with this answer. I wondered, "If we should keep a few commandments, why not the whole of it?" A passion began to burn in me, and through many years of searching, seeking, praying, and studying I came to better understand the spiritual significance of many of the laws, or precepts, of the Torah (the first five books of the Bible) and how I could apply these truths to my life.

Before I go any further, I want to state clearly that my intent in writing this book is not to put anyone under the Law but rather to help us understand the spiritual significance of the Law and its relevance for us today as both Jewish and Gentile followers of Jesus. The Bible makes it plain that we "are not under law but under grace" (Rom. 6:14). But there is a difference in being under the Law versus living by the holy wisdom and instruction it contains.

There is a lot of confusion in the world today, and many sincere believers lack clarity and are unsure how to walk in God's ways. Yet as we will see, the Lord has revealed His ways to us in the Torah. When we view them rightly, God's commands reveal who He is and how we can live holy before Him.

According to Rabbinic Judaism, there are 613 laws in the Torah (also known as the Pentateuch). The 613 commandments, often referred to as *mitzvot*, are not merely rules to be followed but are spiritual treasures designed to bring us closer to our Creator. These laws are not just Jewish traditions; they contain rich blessings that will benefit everyone who applies them in their lives, Jew and Gentile alike.

Judaism teaches that the 613 precepts of the Torah include 365 negative commandments, which coincide with the days of the solar year, and 248 positive commands, symbolizing the number of bones and main organs in the human body. This symbolism that connects the number of laws to the number of bones and organs in our bodies and the number of days in a calendar year illuminates how these laws can be intricately woven into the fabric of our very being and daily lives.

According to Rashi (1010–1105), one of Judaism's most famous Torah commentators, the number 613 is also reflected in the tzitzit (the fringes you see on the four corners of a Jewish prayer shawl). How? Every Hebrew letter has a corresponding numerical value. A few examples of this are that the first letter in the Hebrew alphabet, *alef*, corresponds to the number one. The eleventh letter in the Hebrew alphabet, *kaf*, corresponds to the number twenty. The last letter of the Hebrew alphabet, *tav*, corresponds to the number four hundred. Rashi calculated that in Hebrew the letters that spell out the word *tzitzit* add up to 600. When you add 600 to the eight threads that make up the fringes and the five knots with which the fringes are tied, the total is 613

(600 + 8 + 5). For Orthodox Jews, this makes the tzitzit a constant reminder of God's 613 commandments.[1]

Rabbinic Judaism is very colorful and has many rich analogies that make a point, although not all are objectively or scientifically factual. For example, Judaism teaches that one of Israel's most celebrated fruits, the pomegranate, has 613 seeds in it. (In reality, though, the number of seeds can vary.) Interestingly, however, the robe of the high priest of Israel was decorated with pomegranates! (See Exodus 28:31–34.)

As you may imagine, many of the laws in the Torah cannot be literally observed. For example, because there is no monarchy or king in modern Israel (which some of the laws pertain to) and since slavery has been abolished (which other precepts address), certain commandments are no longer carried out. Furthermore, in AD 70 the Romans besieged Jerusalem and destroyed the Temple. Since many of the laws in the Torah pertain specifically to Temple practices and the duties of the priests who performed their role within it, these laws also can no longer be kept.

This, however, does not diminish the importance of these commandments. Instead, it invites us to understand their deeper revelation and timeless meanings. Each commandment contains a spiritual and moral lesson that can enrich our lives and guide our walk with HaShem (God). Rabbi Yeshua declared, "Do not think that I came to abolish the Law or the Prophets; I did not come to abolish but to fulfill....Whoever then annuls one of the least of these commandments, and teaches others to do the same, shall be called least in the kingdom of heaven; but whoever keeps and teaches them, he shall be called great in the kingdom of heaven" (Matt. 5:17, 19).

Messiah Jesus' teachings and life provide the perfect lens through which we can understand and apply the commandments to our lives today. His fulfillment of the Law does not mean the commandments are rendered obsolete; rather, He brought their ultimate purpose and meaning to light. Through

Messiah, we can see how the commandments point to foundational spiritual truths that lead us into a deeper relationship with our Creator.

Again, one common misconception is that studying and honoring the Torah means putting ourselves under the Law. Let me assure you, this is not the case. As followers of Yeshua we are not under the Law but are led by the Spirit. Messiah Jesus has fulfilled the legal requirements of the Law for us. Our approach to the Torah is not one of legalistic obedience but rather about understanding the essence of the commandments, recognizing that the Law was given to reveal God's character.

Early on in church history, a separation began to take place between Judaism and Christianity. As a result of this growing split, much wrong theology emerged. An example of this can be seen in the translation of John 1:17 in the King James Version (KJV) of the Bible: "For the law was given by Moses, but grace and truth came by Jesus Christ." Notice the word *but.*

But sets up a contrast between two opposites. For example, someone may say to the manager of a restaurant, "The steak was very good, *but* the service was poor." Now think about this as it relates to the translation of John 1:17 in the KJV. By using the word *but,* the translators make it seem as though the law and grace are opposites: "For the law was given by Moses, but grace and truth came by Jesus Christ."

The word *but* in the KJV was added by the translators because of an anti-Jewish mindset, which began infiltrating the church as early as AD 325 under Constantine.[2] As a result, countless numbers of Christians have been taught that the grace of God and the law of God are contrary to each other.

To get the true idea of what the apostle John was communicating, let's take a look at John 1:17, along with the verse that precedes it, from the New American Standard Bible:

> For of His fullness we have all received, and *grace upon grace.* For the Law was given through Moses; grace and truth were realized through Jesus Christ.
>
> —John 1:16–17, emphasis added

Notice there are two graces in verse 16—"grace upon grace." The first grace was the Law. The second grace is the gift of Messiah Jesus, in whom God's grace is fully realized. The Law was a preliminary and preparative grace that elevated God's people out of the sinful culture that surrounded them. But when Messiah Jesus came, God's grace was wholly realized. In fact, Yeshua lived out the laws and commandments in a way that demonstrated love and truth, and in doing so, He showed us that the Law is not a burden but a road map to a life pleasing to God.

The Torah is God's self-disclosure. Jesus, as the full revelation of the Father, upheld the Law and taught its deeper spiritual significance. He challenged us to look beyond the letter of the commandments and embrace their spiritual applications. As He said, "Therefore every scribe who has become a disciple of the kingdom of heaven is like a head of a household, who brings out of his treasure things new and old" (Matt. 13:52). A scribe in Yeshua's day was someone who knew and taught the Torah.

Moreover, Yeshua's fulfillment of the Law opened the way for all people, both Jews and Gentiles, to enter into a covenant relationship with the Creator. The Hebrew prophets Jeremiah and Ezekiel prophesied about the time that would come when God would write His Law upon our hearts by His Spirit (Jer. 31:31–33; Ezek. 36:26–27). Yeshua instituted this prophesied new covenant, and now we are empowered by His Spirit to live out the principles of the commandments in a way that goes beyond external observance to a transformation of the inner person. Thus, as we study these commandments, we do so with the understanding that they are not merely historical relics but living words that continue to speak to us today. They call us to reflect on how we live and love in a modern context. In this light, the commandments become not a set of restrictions but a source of spiritual nourishment and growth, drawing us closer to God and helping us to reflect His character in our lives.

In this book, we will look at more than one hundred of these commandments, delving into what they meant to the ancient Israelites and how they are applicable for us today as Jesus' disciples.

Paul, the Jewish apostle (*shalíach* in Hebrew, meaning "sent one" or "messenger"), wrote that "the Law is holy, and the commandment is holy and righteous and good" and "the Law is spiritual" (Rom. 7:12, 14). Paul taught Timothy that the sacred writings are able to make us wise for salvation and are profitable for teaching, for reproof, for correction, and for training in righteousness (2 Tim. 3:14–16). These verses highlight the value of the Law when approached with the right heart and understanding. This is why Paul penned, "The Law is good, if one uses it lawfully" (1 Tim. 1:8).

Before we get into the individual laws, I want to mention that in these pages I use the terms *commandment*, *precept*, *law*, and *mitzvah*—a Hebrew word meaning precept or commandment—interchangeably. In addition, I employ a variety of terms to refer to God, including Adonai (Lord), Yahweh (God's personal name), Elohim (the title of the Creator used in Genesis), the Most High, the Blessed One, and HaShem (Hebrew for "the Name"). At times these terms shed light on who God is, and I hope that in using them, you will be blessed and that Gentile followers of Yeshua will become better acquainted with them.

I also occasionally refer to believers in Jesus as followers of "The Way." This goes back to the Book of Acts, where five separate times Jesus' followers were referred to in this way. For example, in Acts 9:1–2 we read (ESV, emphasis added):

> But Saul, still breathing threats and murder against the disciples of the Lord, went to the high priest and asked him for letters to the synagogues at Damascus, so that if he found any belonging to *the Way*, men or women, he might bring them bound to Jerusalem.

Ultimately, this book aims to bridge the gap between the ancient commandments of the Torah and our contemporary lives. Whether you are Jewish or Gentile, I hope this will be an epic biblical exploration that will enrich your faith and deepen your relationship with your Creator. Let us walk this path together, discovering the treasures of the Torah while at the same time rejoicing in our salvation through Yeshua HaMashiach.

Shalom,

Rabbi Schneider

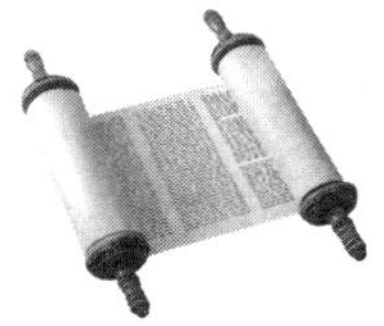

TO BE FRUITFUL AND MULTIPLY, AND FILL THE EARTH AND SUBDUE IT

God blessed them; and God said to them, "Be fruitful and multiply, and fill the earth, and subdue it; and rule over the fish of the sea and over the birds of the sky and over every living thing that moves on the earth."
—GENESIS 1:28

THIS VERSE REVEALS God's first and foundational commandment to humanity: to be *fruitful, multiply, and fill the earth.* Whether Jew or Gentile, the first calling of all humans is to reproduce—to create families, communities, and nations that thrive under the leadership of God the Creator; obey His commands; and enjoy His blessings.

The ancient Israelites saw the mandate to be fruitful and multiply as essential for the continuation of their nation and the fulfillment of God's covenant promises. It was a call to grow in numbers and spread God's rule and blessings throughout the earth.

The command to be fruitful and multiply continues to resonate within the Jewish community today. In particular, one reason Orthodox Jews still have so many children is to repopulate the earth with Jewish souls after the loss of six million Jews during the Holocaust, showing that this mitzvah is still at the forefront of Orthodox Jewish thinking.

This directive not only pertains to physical reproduction but also addresses humanity's responsibility to steward the earth and exercise dominion over all living creatures. The command to "rule over" the fish of the sea, the birds of the sky, and every living creature positions humans as vice-regents of God as we exercise His delegated authority over creation. Our dominion mandate requires us to compassionately care for all living beings, reflecting Adonai's character and love for His creation.

From a New Testament perspective, we find a spiritual application deeply rooted in the concept of bearing the fruit of the Spirit and expanding the domain of the kingdom of God. Just as humanity is called to multiply *physically*, believers as a whole—both Jew and Gentile alike—are called to multiply *spiritually* by sharing the message of salvation and making disciples of all nations. (See Matthew 28:19–20.) Additionally, through the indwelling of the Holy Spirit, believers are empowered to bear the fruit of love, joy, peace, patience, kindness, goodness, faithfulness, gentleness, and self-control (Gal. 5:22–23).

The command to "be fruitful and multiply, and fill the earth, and subdue it" (Gen. 1:28) reveals the glory and responsibility of mankind, who has been created in God's own image. By expanding in numbers and godly influence while stewarding everything under our authority, we are fulfilling God's purpose for our lives.

CIRCUMCISION

This is My covenant, which you shall keep, between Me and you and your descendants after you: every male among you shall be circumcised.
—Genesis 17:10

Circumcision was a central facet of God's covenant with Abraham and his descendants. Through circumcision individuals outwardly demonstrated their allegiance to Adonai's commandments and covenantal promises. As members of God's first covenant people, the Israelite men appeared different physically because of this visible mark. Other nations recognized the Israelites were a people set apart and holy to God, a people among whom God Himself would live and move (Lev. 26:12).

This ancient ritual, deeply embedded in Jewish tradition, transcended mere physicality to embody a spiritual commitment to God's commandments and covenantal promises. Through the act of circumcision individuals outwardly demonstrated their allegiance to the community and their unwavering dedication to the divine covenant established with Abraham. Circumcision profoundly symbolized the cutting away of sinful inclinations and fleshly desires to embrace a life characterized by devotion to God and spiritual purity. By undergoing circumcision, the Israelites were set apart as a sanctified nation, called to embody God's righteousness and serve as a beacon of light to the nations, as foretold in Isaiah 42:6.

In the same way, our lives should clearly show the world that we are set apart and different—not because of a physical difference but because of a spiritual one. The physical distinction that so marked Abraham and his descendants foretold a deeper and more permanent work of the Spirit: the cutting away of worldly motivations and values. Paul referred to this in Romans 2:29 as a circumcision of the heart by the Spirit, writing, "Nor is circumcision that which is outward in the flesh. But…circumcision is that which is of the heart, by the Spirit, not by the letter" (Rom. 2:28–29).

While there continues to be value in physical circumcision for the Jewish people, believers are called to transform the Israelites' outward circumcision into a spiritual one—so our lives are characterized by holiness, purity, and separation from the world. Just as circumcision distinguished the Israelites from other nations, believers as a whole are summoned to be a holy people, set apart for the divine purposes of proclaiming God's glory and advancing His kingdom on earth (1 Pet. 2:9).

Paul spoke of this spiritual circumcision in his letter to the Galatian churches, writing that this physical sign did not justify a person under the new covenant. Rather, God used that practice to prophesy that one day we would be set apart spiritually in our inner man. Again, our "circumcision" would be a condition of the heart. This was accomplished by Messiah Yeshua on the cross, as Paul wrote, "For in Christ Jesus neither circumcision nor uncircumcision means anything, but faith working through love" (Gal. 5:6).

On a practical level, most followers of Yeshua today know there is no spiritual requirement on Gentile believers to be physically circumcised. But in Paul's day, some Jewish believers in Jesus were falling into the error of placing higher value on physical circumcision than on the spiritual principle to which this law points. Some even used physical circumcision to promote their own ministries!

Paul wrote:

> For those who are circumcised do not even keep the Law themselves, but they desire to have you circumcised so that they may boast in your flesh. But may it never be that I would boast, except in the cross of our Lord Jesus Christ, through which the world has been crucified to me, and I to the world. For neither is circumcision anything, nor uncircumcision, but a new creation. And those who will walk by this rule, peace and mercy be upon them, and upon the Israel of God.
>
> —Galatians 6:13–16

Through the inward circumcision of the heart, empowered by the Holy Spirit, believers are equipped to live in a way that bears witness to our allegiance to God and reflects His character to a watching world. Thus, the command regarding circumcision (Gen. 17:10) calls us who have been circumcised in the heart by the Messiah to walk in obedience, reflecting the reality that we have been separated from the world unto God.

THE PROHIBITION AGAINST EATING THE THIGH MUSCLE OF ANY ANIMAL

Therefore, to this day the sons of Israel do not eat the sinew of the hip which is on the socket of the thigh, because he touched the socket of Jacob's thigh in the sinew of the hip.
—Genesis 32:32

In Genesis 32, Jacob was in a moment of great crisis. He was about to meet his twin brother, Esau, twenty years after he had fled from him because of Esau's murderous intentions. Still fearing for his life, Jacob divided his flocks, sent them ahead as gifts, and bedded down on the ground with a rock as his pillow for what he thought might be the last night of his life. There, at a place he later called Beth El, the House of God, he experienced one of the most profound revelations of God to be found in the entire Bible.

That night, God came to Jacob in the form of a man and wrestled with him until daybreak. Before departing from him, God touched Jacob's hip socket and dislocated it permanently. Afterward, in this same encounter, God changed Jacob's name to Israel and blessed him (Gen. 32:24–43).

What does this have to do with you and me as followers of The Way? As Paul might have put it, much in every way! You see, by touching Jacob's hip, God demonstrated that His greatest power operates in the midst of our most glaring and painful weaknesses.

God blessed Jacob only after dislocating his hip. From that moment on, Jacob, the father of the twelve patriarchs, limped.

Bereshit Rabbah, the ancient Jewish exegesis on the Book of Genesis, offers this insight: "The thigh is the seat of pride. The Holy One, blessed be He, said to Jacob: 'You rely on your thigh? I will strike it!'" This commentary highlights the symbolism behind Jacob's struggle with the angel, portraying it as a metaphorical battle against pride and self-reliance. The clear lesson for us is that before God can use us in His highest purposes, He must break us in order to bring us to the place of fully relying on Him. Again, Jacob's physical disablement serves as a metaphorical gateway to spiritual transformation, symbolizing the necessity of being humbled before receiving divine favor.

Paul's reflection on this theme in 2 Corinthians 12:9–10 further illuminates the principle. Having begged God three times to relieve him of a tormenting "messenger of Satan," Paul received a surprising response: "[My] power is perfected in weakness." Why did Messiah respond to Paul in this way? Paul explained, "To keep me from exalting myself."

Like Jacob, Paul had experienced unprecedented heavenly visions and visitations. Like Jacob, Paul was chosen to bring unusually great blessings to the believing community and the earth. But the frailty of fallen human nature—that is, our tendency toward pride—requires that we be constantly reminded we are but humble creatures.

Both Jacob and Paul benefited from painful weaknesses so they could bear the glory of their respective revelations faithfully and fulfill their divine callings. In this manner, God demonstrated great strength through both men without driving them into self-exaltation. Through Paul's lens, weakness becomes not a hindrance but a pathway to experiencing the fullness of God's grace. In essence, Paul embraces vulnerability so Yeshua's power will be made manifest in and through him.

This principle can be readily applied in our everyday lives: To walk in God's best for us and accomplish all He has planned for us, we must be willing to walk humbly, with a limp. We must accept many of the trials we face in life as opportunities for God's strength to be made perfect in our weakness. Paul embraced this principle so fully that he wrote: "Most gladly, therefore, I will rather boast about my weaknesses, so that the power of Christ may dwell in me. Therefore I am well content with weaknesses, with insults, with distresses, with persecutions, with difficulties, for Christ's sake; for when I am weak, then I am strong" (2 Cor. 12:9–10).

I would add another point here, which some rabbinic commentators have drawn out, and it is that no one should let a physical handicap stop or discourage them. Rabbinic teachings often emphasize the importance of resilience and perseverance despite physical limitations. Jacob continued to "wrestle with God" despite his dislocated hip, and he prevailed. He also lived out his destiny to be the father of the tribes of Israel and was named in the Hebrews 11 "hall of faith."

Rabbinic commentators use Jacob's example of persisting in his struggle with Yahweh, even after sustaining a debilitating injury, to point out the importance of unwavering faith and determination in the face of adversity. Paul, too, suffered a physical malady yet soldiered on to write much of the New Testament and establish many churches. This is a valid interpretation for those with physical challenges—and for those without. No matter what afflictions we face, God's purposes in us can fully prevail. As we reflect on the prohibition against eating an animal's thigh muscle (Gen. 32:32), may it remind us to embrace the things that make us feel or appear weak, because they can lead to our greatest victories.

THE SANCTIFICATION OF THE MONTH ISRAEL WAS DELIVERED OUT OF EGYPT AS THE FIRST MONTH OF THE YEAR

This month shall be the beginning of months for you;
it is to be the first month of the year to you.
—Exodus 12:2

More than a mere calendar adjustment, this directive instructs the people of Israel to mark their liberation from slavery as the moment of their spiritual rebirth. Israel's identity as a nation preceded their physical deliverance from Egypt, but their true birth as a redeemed people came through their obedience to God's commandment regarding Passover. On that defining night, when they were redeemed by the blood of the Passover lamb placed on their doorposts, Yahweh proclaimed for them a new, national spiritual birthday.

Moreover, Exodus 12:2 helps us to understand the spiritual significance of *time* in the Scriptures. By designating the month of the Israelites' deliverance as the beginning of the year, God established a framework for His people to commemorate and reflect on His redemptive acts. With each new year, the Israelites would be reminded of Adonai's faithfulness and provision, which would anchor them in their identity as a liberated people.

Similarly, for believers in Yeshua, marking significant personal spiritual milestones, such as when we decided to follow

Jesus, as well as God's biblical holidays as outlined in Leviticus 23—Shabbat, Passover, the Feast of Unleavened Bread, the Feast of Firstfruits, Pentecost, the Feast of Trumpets, the Day of Atonement, and the Feast of Tabernacles—reminds us of Father God's faithfulness to us and His transforming power at work in our lives. These remembrances can then become moments of deep encounter with God and serve to reaffirm our commitment to Him.

Notice also that while this mitzvah is given to the nation of Israel as a whole, its implications extend to every Israelite individually. In order for the entire nation to keep this command to sanctify the first month, each Israelite had to recognize and celebrate it. Thus, each person contributed to the overall identity and strength of the nation. In much the same way, every believer's spiritual birth and vigor contributes to the overall identity and strength of the body of Messiah. In this sense, the command to the entire nation of Israel to corporately sanctify the month of their deliverance from Egypt as the first month of the year (Exod. 12:2) serves as a prophetic call to unity for the body of Messiah.

ALL OF ISRAEL WAS TO PARTICIPATE IN SLAUGHTERING THE FIRST PASSOVER LAMB

The whole assembly of the congregation of Israel is to kill it at twilight.
—Exodus 12:6

This commandment again reveals the communal nature of the Passover observance, placing great importance on the collective responsibility of the entire nation by giving each member a role to play in the sacrifice, symbolizing their unity as a people and their shared covenant with God.

The fact that "the whole assembly of the congregation of Israel" was to kill the Passover lamb reminded them that their redemption was personal as well as collective because every individual was involved. The law connected each individual to the sacrifice that rescued them from the angel of death, which killed every firstborn son of both man and beast. So too does this command connect each of us as followers of The Way to the sacrifice that rescued us from death.

The sacrifice of the Passover lamb finds its ultimate fulfillment in the person of Yeshua, "the Lamb of God who takes away the sin of the world" (John 1:29). Messiah Jesus willingly offered Himself as the sacrificial Lamb, fulfilling the requirements of the Mosaic Law and providing redemption for humanity's sins. His death on the cross and the pouring out of His blood represent the ultimate act of love and atonement for believers. Thus, in a profound and personal way, every individual who receives Yeshua as Savior participates in His sacrificial death, recognizing that it was for them specifically that He died.

Just as the Israelites were instructed to actively partake in the Passover lamb's slaughter, so we as believers in Yeshua are invited to spiritually identify with Messiah Jesus' death. Through faith in Him, we acknowledge our role in His sacrifice and embrace the forgiveness and redemption offered through His shed blood. Yeshua allowed Himself to be put to death because He loved you and me, directly and personally. We each played a part in putting Him to death because it was for us that He died. This shared experience of salvation unites believers across cultural and ethnic boundaries, fulfilling the prophetic foreshadowing of the Passover lamb and affirming our common identity as the redeemed people of God.

Further, the communal aspect of the Passover sacrifice serves as a poignant reminder of the interconnectedness of the body of believers in Messiah Yeshua. Just as the Israelites came together as a community to partake in the Passover observance, so we are called to participate as a community in Communion.

The fact that the Passover lamb was to be slaughtered at twilight also carries profound significance, as it points to the darkness that enveloped the land during Yeshua's crucifixion. In the Gospel accounts, Jesus was crucified on Passover at the ninth hour, approximately 3 p.m., coinciding with the time of the evening sacrifice in the Temple.

> It was now about the sixth hour, and darkness fell over the whole land until the ninth hour, because the sun was obscured; and the veil of the temple was torn in two. And Jesus, crying out with a loud voice, said, "Father, into Your hands I commit

> My spirit." Having said this, He breathed His last.
>
> —Luke 23:44–46; see also Matthew 27:45–50 and Mark 15:33–37

This again shows that Yeshua is the Messianic fulfillment of the Passover lamb. Through His death and resurrection Yeshua inaugurated a new covenant that offers forgiveness and redemption to all who believe in Him. May the precept calling all of Israel to participate in slaughtering the first Passover lamb (Exod. 12:6) remind us that Yeshua is indeed "the Lamb of God who takes away the sin of the world" (John 1:29).

NONE OF THE UNEATEN PASSOVER LAMB COULD BE LEFT UNTIL MORNING

And you shall not leave any of it over until morning, but whatever is left of it until morning, you shall burn with fire.
—Exodus 12:10

You shall not offer the blood of My sacrifice with leavened bread; nor is the fat of My feast to remain overnight until morning.
—Exodus 23:18

This commandment highlighted the importance of treating the Passover sacrifice with reverence and ensuring its proper disposal. By consuming the entire lamb or discarding its remnants through burning, the Israelites demonstrated their obedience to God's instructions and honored the sanctity of the Passover meal, which was necessary for their salvation and deliverance.

Prophetically, this law illuminates and points to the importance of fully embracing the beauty and value of Messiah Jesus, who is the supreme Lamb of God. Just as the Israelites were instructed not to let any part of the lamb go to waste, we are called to fully appropriate the saving work of Mashiach (the Anointed One) in our lives. We are to honor Yeshua's sacrifice by walking in wholehearted devotion to Him and surrendering ourselves completely to His lordship.

Even as the Israelites were commanded to consume the Pesach

(Passover) lamb in its entirety, so are we to receive Jesus fully and completely into our lives—not just to taste Him, compartmentalize our relationship with Him, or add Him on to our daily routines. It is for this reason Yeshua said in Revelation 3:16 that He spits the lukewarm out of His mouth. We are to remember this each time we take Communion and symbolically eat His flesh and drink His blood in identification with the Passover lamb.

Only after the Israelites fully consumed the lamb could they exit Egypt and enter into freedom, and only when we fully consume Yeshua's life can we enter the wholeness and freedom Messiah Jesus wants us to have in Him. The command that none of the uneaten Passover lamb be left until morning (Exod. 12:10; 23:18) shines new light on this reality.

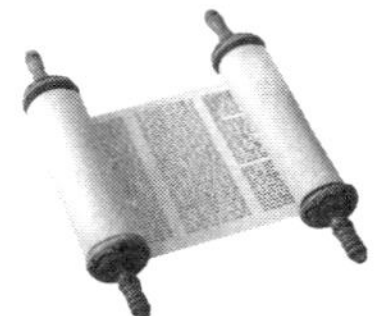

NONE OF THE BONES OF THE PASSOVER LAMB COULD BE BROKEN

It is to be eaten in a single house; you are not to bring forth any of the flesh outside of the house, nor are you to break any bone of it.
—Exodus 12:46

This law—reiterated in Numbers 9:12—calls attention to the importance of preserving the integrity of the sacrificial lamb and not causing it unnecessary harm. It again highlights the respect due to the Passover sacrifice and the need to preserve its completeness.

Because Yeshua fulfills the Torah, none of His bones were broken. John 19:36 (MEV) tells us "that the Scripture should be fulfilled, 'Not one of His bones shall be broken.'" In this verse, John was referring to the fact that when Jesus was crucified, the Roman soldiers refrained from breaking His legs as they broke the legs of the two criminals crucified with Him. This, of course, fulfilled Exodus 12:46 and pointed to Jesus' identity as the ultimate Passover Lamb.

The preservation of the Passover lamb's bones also symbolizes the completeness of the sacrifice. In contrast to the way sacrificial animals were mutilated in pagan rituals, the Passover lamb was to be offered whole and unblemished, reflecting God's standard of perfect purity and holiness. Because Yeshua's atoning work on the cross is complete and perfect, believers are made whole, receiving forgiveness and total reconciliation to the Holy One.

Interestingly, some rabbinic commentators interpret this law as symbolizing royalty and spiritual elevation. They suggest that through the redemption obtained through the Passover lamb the children of Israel became royal kings, and royalty refrains from primitive eating practices like breaking a sacrificed animal's bones to suck out its marrow. Correspondingly, we who partake of Yeshua become kings and priests, as Revelation 1:6 states: "He has made us to be a kingdom, priests." Our lives are refined by the Ruach HaKodesh (Spirit of God), and as royalty, we follow a higher and more excellent way.

As we reflect on the mitzvah that the bones of the Passover lamb could not be broken (Exod. 12:46) and its fulfillment in Yeshua, let us consider the completeness and perfection of His atoning work on the cross and strive to honor His sacrifice by giving Him the best and finest of our lives.

THE BAN ON LEAVEN DURING PASSOVER

Seven days you shall eat unleavened bread, but on the first day you shall remove leaven from your houses; for whoever eats anything leavened from the first day until the seventh day, that person shall be cut off from Israel.
—Exodus 12:15

This law commanding the removal of leaven from the Israelites' homes during Passover speaks of spiritual purification and symbolizes a separating from defilement. By purging their homes of leaven each year at Passover, Israel is to demonstrate their desire to be set apart unto God, free from contamination.

As the Jewish people meticulously rid their homes of leaven, so believers are called to inspect their lives, to identify areas of spiritual impurity or disobedience and remove them. Just as leaven permeates and transforms dough, so can sin infiltrate and corrupt the believer's whole life if left unchecked. Through confession and repentance we can experience cleansing, spiritual renewal, and the joy of salvation.

While leaven is symbolic of all sin, it especially symbolizes pride. The rabbis teach, "The characteristic of leavened dough (Chametz) is that it rises and swells, symbolizing pride and boastfulness. A Matzah [matzo, unleavened bread], on the other hand, is thin and flat, suggesting meekness and humility."[3]

Paul wrote in 1 Corinthians 5:6, "Your boasting is not good.

Do you not know that a little leaven leavens the whole lump of dough?" This mitzvah reminds us that we cannot walk in fellowship with God with pride in our hearts. In Rabbi Yeshua's parable in Luke 18 it was the humble sinner who beat his hands on his heart, saying, "Forgive me, a sinner," who came into alignment with the Creator, not the Pharisee, who had religious pride. This law serves as a pointed reminder that as believers we are called to, in true humility, acknowledge our need for God's grace and forgiveness.

As we consider the command to remove leaven during Passover (Exod. 12:15), let us embrace the call to root everything out of our hearts and lives that offends and displeases God.

THE SANCTIFICATION OF THE FIRSTBORN OF BOTH HUMANS AND ANIMALS

Sanctify to Me every firstborn, the first offspring of every womb among the sons of Israel, both of man and beast; it belongs to Me.
—Exodus 13:2

THIS LAW MANDATES the sanctification of every firstborn, both human and animal, among the sons of Israel. By dedicating the firstborn to God, the Israelites acknowledged His sovereignty and ownership over every aspect of their lives.

Rabbi Moses Maimonides (1138–1204), a great medieval Jewish scholar also referred to as Rambam, taught that this pronouncement first applied "specifically to the firstborn who were alive at the time of the Exodus. In celebration of the fact that they were saved while the Egyptian firstborn were all killed in the final plague, the Israelite firstborn became sanctified."[4] Likewise, we who have been saved from the wrath of God are called to prioritize the kingdom of God and His righteousness above all other aspirations and pursuits.

Rabbi Yeshua taught this principle in Matthew 6:33, instructing His disciples to seek *first* the kingdom of God. In fact, it was a major theme in His parables.

> Again, the kingdom of heaven is like a merchant seeking fine pearls, and upon finding one pearl of great value, he went and

> sold all that he had and bought it.
>
> —Matthew 13:45–46

This command leads us to examine our attitudes toward ownership. By demanding the sanctification of the firstborn, God asserts His rights over everything in our lives. This law spotlights the fact that all our possessions, priorities, and desires ultimately belong to the Most High and must be placed under subjection and in service to His will.

As we reflect on this law regarding the sanctification of the firstborn (Exod. 13:2), may it challenge us to place our will and whole being into the hands of our Maker and surrender all to Him.

TO SHARE THE STORY OF THE EXODUS WITH OUR CHILDREN

You shall tell your son on that day, saying, "It is because of what the LORD did for me when I came out of Egypt."
—EXODUS 13:8

THIS MITZVAH COMMANDS the Israelites to tell their children the story of the Exodus, affirming the importance of passing down the account of redemption from one generation to the next. This directive particularly points to the pivotal role of parents and guardians in transmitting faith and spiritual heritage to their children, reflecting a deeply ingrained Jewish tradition.

Maimonides taught that retelling the Exodus story preserves continuity and communal memory, ensuring the preservation of Jewish identity and faith across generations. By recounting God's miraculous deliverance of the Israelites from bondage, parents ensure their children understand and appreciate Yahweh's saving acts in history and their own identity as members of a chosen people. They also instill in their children a deep trust in the Holy One's promises and a sense of gratitude for His ongoing presence and intervention in their lives.

The act of passing down the Exodus story engendered a sense of belonging and community among the ancient Israelites and continues to do so among Jewish people today. As families gather to recount the story each year at Passover, they strengthen their bonds with one another and affirm their shared identity as a called-out, covenant people.

For followers of The Way, this law carries a significant message about our responsibility to share our stories of redemption with the succeeding generations and specifically calls us to personally engage and invest in the spiritual upbringing of our children. Just as the Israelites were instructed to tell their children about the Exodus, as believers, we are called to teach God's Word and share our own testimonies of God's faithfulness with our offspring.

This law calling the Israelites to share the story of the Exodus with their children (Exod. 13:8) sets before us the importance of *generational transmission* of our faith and spiritual heritage. We are obligated to do more than take our kids to church. We are called to personally share our love for Messiah with them. By telling about our own journeys of faith and modeling a godly life before our sons, daughters, and grandchildren, we can help them catch by osmosis a vibrant and enduring faith.

TO BELIEVE IN GOD'S EXISTENCE AND THAT THERE IS ONLY ONE TRUE GOD

I am the LORD your God, who brought you out of
the land of Egypt, out of the house of slavery.
—EXODUS 20:2

THIS LAW, THE first of the Ten Commandments, calls for belief in the existence of God and serves as the cornerstone of monotheism. It also set the terms for the covenant relationship between Yahweh and Israel, because implicit in this declaration is Adonai's total claim over His people and their consequent commitment to obeying Him. By acknowledging God as the one who brought them out of the land of Egypt, out of the house of slavery, the Israelites affirmed His supremacy and the central role He was to have in their lives and community.

Within this law we also see the personal nature of God's relationship with His first covenant, chosen people. By identifying Himself as "the LORD your God," the Lord speaks in intimate terms of His connection with the people of Israel and His ongoing involvement in their lives. This is not a distant and uninvolved deity but a God who knows His people by name, hears their cries, and acts on their behalf. Thus, this commandment is not merely a statement of Yahweh's authority but a declaration of His love and fidelity, which demanded a response from Israel. By pledging their allegiance to God alone, the Israelites entered a sacred covenant with Him, bound by guarantees that required obedience and promised blessing. This covenantal relationship forms the basis of Israel's identity as a chosen people and sets them apart from the surrounding nations.

Contrast this mitzvah to believe that God exists, that there is only one true God, and that He must be obeyed, honored, and loved with the words of the apostle Paul in Romans 1:18–25, where he describes the consequences of rejecting the Creator:

> For the wrath of God is revealed from heaven against all ungodliness and unrighteousness of men who suppress the truth in unrighteousness, because that which is known about God is evident within them; for God made it evident to them. For since the creation of the world His invisible attributes, His eternal power and divine nature, have been clearly seen, being understood through what has been made, so that they are without excuse. For even though they knew God, they did not honor Him as God or give thanks, but they became futile in their speculations, and their foolish heart was darkened.
>
> Professing to be wise, they became fools, and exchanged the glory of the incorruptible God for an image in the form of corruptible man and of birds and four-footed animals and crawling creatures. Therefore God gave them over in the lusts of their hearts to impurity, so that their bodies would be dishonored among them. For they exchanged the truth of God for a lie, and worshiped and served the creature rather than the Creator, who is blessed forever.

By considering Exodus 20:2 in light of Paul's words in Romans 1:18–25, we see with clarity the importance of acknowledging Yahweh, the Father of Jesus, as the one true God and submitting to His authority. Just as the Israelites were called to recognize the Most High's sovereignty and obey His commandments, so we today must affirm God's existence and honor Him as the Master and Ruler of all things or face the consequences.

A person who refuses to acknowledge Elohim as the omniscient, omnipotent, omnipresent Creator and the first cause of all things has broken the foundation of all God's laws. The Holy One must be accepted as our Lord and King who has total claim to our lives. He is to be loved as a personal God, not just some cosmic force.

The command to believe God exists and that there is only one true God (Exod. 20:2) should permeate our consciousness and affect our lives at the deepest level. We must see Him as a personal God who wants to be involved in our daily lives and will intervene in our circumstances, just as He intervened on His people Israel's behalf by bringing them out of bondage in Egypt.

TO BELIEVE IN NO DIVINITY BUT GOD

You shall have no other gods before Me.
—Exodus 20:3

In a world filled with competing idols, Yahweh boldly stakes His claim for the Israelites' complete devotion by commanding their full allegiance.

Like the precept in Exodus 20:2, this law establishes a monotheistic foundation by forbidding the worship of any other gods within the covenant community. But this mitzvah addresses more than the act of bowing or sacrificing to statues or graven images. It delves into the heart issue of idolatry.

"Other gods" can be anything in which we place our confidence or devotion. For some, it may be placing undue importance on higher education or professional success, relying inordinately on human wisdom, or even idolizing family members or certain relationships. For others, it may be medical expertise or seeking acceptance from the world. Others have broken this commandment by seeking to know the future through fortune-telling, astrology, or other forbidden means. None of these can bring the happiness and contentment we desire, and they will ultimately lead us into bondage. This is why Paul said, "Therefore, my beloved, flee from idolatry" (1 Cor. 10:14).

This law to believe in no other God (Exod. 20:3) challenges us to examine our hearts and commit to trusting God above all else, seeking Him alone to meet our needs and satisfy our desires. Just as the Israelites were commanded to have no other gods before Yahweh, believers today are called to reject all forms of idolatry and keep the Lord alone at the center of our lives.

TO MAKE NO GRAVEN IMAGES IN GOD'S LIKENESS

You shall not make for yourself an idol [graven image], or any likeness of what is in heaven above or on the earth beneath or in the water under the earth.
—Exodus 20:4

By prohibiting the creation of graven images, or idols, this commandment serves as a bulwark against the temptation to reduce the infinite and transcendent God to a finite and material form, and reminds God's people of the spiritual nature of their relationship with Him.

In ancient Near Eastern cultures the worship of physical idols pervaded society, with various gods and goddesses represented by statues and images. These idols were believed to embody a divine presence and were worshipped accordingly. Thus, the prohibition against graven images served many purposes within the Israelite community.

First, it distinguished their worship from that of neighboring cultures and illuminated the uniqueness of the Holy One of Israel, the authentic God. While other nations relied on physical representations to interact with their deities, the Israelites were instructed to worship a personal God who was invisible.

Second, the command served as a safeguard against idolatry. Throughout their history the Israelites faced the temptation to worship false gods, often succumbing to the pressures of cultural assimilation and political expediency. Distressing circumstances also made the Israelites vulnerable to fall into idol worship, as was the case when they made a golden calf at Mount Sinai because Moses had not come down from the mountain. Not knowing where he was, they panicked and resorted to idol worship. The law against graven images called them back to affirming their exclusive allegiance to the God of their forefathers and the fundamental principle of monotheism.

This precept also served as a reminder that while the gods of other nations were depicted in human or animal form, the God of Israel could not be similarly represented. He was beyond human comprehension, existing outside the limitations of time and space. Therefore, any attempt to depict God in material form would inevitably fall short of capturing His true nature. The commandment, then, challenged the Israelites to acknowledge God's transcendence and approach Him with humility and reverence.

Today, some followers of Yeshua continue to be tempted to venerate statues and pictures of Jesus. While these works of art may be intended to inspire devotion and reverence, they carry the risk of detracting from the true person of worship, who is God alone. By creating physical representations, believers may inadvertently engage in idolatry, placing undue emphasis on the created object rather than the Creator.

Thus, this precept to make no graven images in God's likeness (Exod. 20:4) challenges us to reject graven images and cultivate a deep, intimate relationship with our Maker. It calls us to worship Him in spirit and truth, acknowledging His transcendence and holiness. By doing this, we not only avoid idolatry; we magnify the one true God and affirm our commitment to Him.

TO NOT TAKE THE LORD'S NAME IN VAIN

You shall not take the name of the LORD your God in vain, for the LORD will not leave him unpunished who takes His name in vain.
—EXODUS 20:7

THIS COMMAND WARNS against profaning God's name, underlining the seriousness of this offense by warning believers that God will punish those who dishonor His name.

Names held great significance in ancient Near Eastern cultures. A person's name was believed to embody his essence and identity. Therefore, invoking someone's name carried great weight and authority. Similarly, in the Hebrew worldview, God's name was and is considered sacred, pure, and holy. God's personal name, Yahweh—comprised of the Hebrew consonants *yod, hey, vav, hey,* which are represented by the tetragrammaton YHWH—was and is still so revered that it is often not pronounced out of respect for its holiness. Instead, titles such as Adonai (Lord) or Elohim (God) are used to refer to Him. Therefore, the commandment against taking the name of the Lord in vain was not merely about avoiding profanity or blasphemy; it was about acknowledging the sacredness of God's name. It is a call to treat God's name with the utmost respect and honor.

New covenant believers should understand that there are various ways in which God's name is taken in vain. One involves the misuse of His name in oaths or vows, which Yeshua cautioned against in Matthew 5:34–37: "Make no oath at all, either by heaven, for it is the throne of God, or by the earth, for it is the footstool of His feet, or by Jerusalem, for it is the city of the great King....But let your statement be, 'Yes, yes' or 'No, no'; anything beyond these is of evil."

Whether a person is promising that he is telling the truth, will never do something again, or will keep a secret (such as by saying, "I swear to God"), swearing in God's name is forbidden. Again, Jesus called it evil and admonished believers to let their yes be yes and their no be no, avoiding the need for oaths altogether.

Tossing God's name around flippantly in casual conversation or, even worse, using it as a swear word reflects a lack of the holy fear of the Lord and disregard for His sacredness.

Beyond cautioning against verbal oaths or vows, this mitzvah prohibiting taking the Lord's name in vain (Exod. 20:7) encompasses the broader concept of representing God well to the world. As God's ambassadors, believers bear the responsibility of reflecting His character and nature to those around us. Some have rejected or been turned off to Messiah Jesus because He has been misrepresented by His people. Any actions or words that bring dishonor to God's name are a violation of this commandment.

TO REMEMBER AND KEEP THE SABBATH

Remember the sabbath day, to keep it holy. Six days you shall labor and do all your work, but the seventh day is a sabbath of the Lord your God; in it you shall not do any work, you or your son or your daughter, your male or your female servant or your cattle or your sojourner who stays with you. For in six days the Lord made the heavens and the earth, the sea and all that is in them, and rested on the seventh day; therefore the Lord blessed the sabbath day and made it holy.

—Exodus 20:8–11

Rather than being a legalistic tradition, honoring the Sabbath is a principle of creation established in the beginning. This sacred day of rest, set apart by God, predates the Mosaic Law and applies to all people, Jews and Gentiles alike.

We read in the Book of Genesis, or Bereshit ("in the beginning") in Hebrew, "By the seventh day God completed His work which He had done, and He rested on the seventh day from all His work which He had done. Then God blessed the seventh day and sanctified it, because in it He rested from all His work which God had created and made" (Gen. 2:2–3).

Here we see that at creation God sanctified the seventh day, establishing it as holy and instituting a pattern of rest. The Sabbath, then, reflects God's inherent wisdom in providing a rhythm of work and rest for humanity, acknowledging our need for physical, mental, and spiritual rejuvenation. By observing the

Sabbath, we recognize God's sovereignty over time and align our lives with His divine order for each week, which helps us to maintain balance in our lives.

Many people think they're too busy to step back and recharge, but ignoring the cycles of rest Father God instituted through the Sabbath leads to less productivity and eventually burnout. In the New Testament, Yeshua reaffirms the enduring relevance of the Sabbath, saying in Mark 2, "The Sabbath was made for man, and not man for the Sabbath. So the Son of Man is Lord even of the Sabbath" (vv. 27–28). The Sabbath is a gift bestowed on humanity to serve and bless us. Far from being a burdensome duty, honoring the Sabbath is a means of bringing restoration.

The Sabbath presents a timeless invitation to pause—*selah*—reflect, and reconnect with God to receive respite from the demands of daily life and be rejuvenated physically and spiritually. It is an invitation to cultivate deeper intimacy with God by entering His rest and experiencing the fullness of His presence. In addition to the Sabbath being the sign of the covenant between God and Israel (Exod. 31:13), it is an opportunity to bring spiritual blessing to all of humanity.

In a world marked by busyness and distraction, the command to remember and keep the Sabbath (Exod. 20:8–11) stands as a countercultural directive, challenging each of us to prioritize our relationship with God by honoring the cycle of rest He established and built into creation.

Every time we observe and remember the Sabbath, we are affirming that Elohim created the world. If the whole world celebrated the Sabbath, there would be no agnostics or atheists.

TO HONOR YOUR FATHER AND MOTHER

Honor your father and your mother, that your days may be prolonged in the land which the LORD your God gives you.
—EXODUS 20:12

THE COMMANDMENT TO honor one's father and mother is woven inextricably into the moral and spiritual fabric of human existence. In Judaism, honoring our parents is considered an act of worshipping God. The Talmud—a central text of Rabbinic Judaism and a primary source of Jewish religious law, customs, and history[5]—teaches that there are three partners in the formation of a person: father, mother, and the Almighty. In honoring our father and mother, we are acknowledging God's partnership with them in creating us and His care of us through them.

This mitzvah is part of the Ten Commandments, which outline the foundational principles for walking in alignment with the Creator. It emphasizes the importance of familial relationships and the role of parents as stewards of God's authority in the lives of their children. By honoring our parents, we acknowledge the order established by God and affirm our commitment to living in harmony with His will.

Honoring our father and mother extends beyond merely obeying them to include having a deep sense of reverence, gratitude, and compassion toward them. Honoring them can involve giving affection as a way of expressing gratitude for their guidance, wisdom, and love. It may look like cherishing the memories shared together and carrying forward the practical and spiritual lessons they imparted. When we honor our parents, we show appreciation for the sacrifices they made to provide for us in our infancy and youth, and we set an example for our children to care for and honor us in our old age. In doing this, our "days may be prolonged," as this mitzvah says.

However, I realize not everyone has experienced parental love and support. Many have endured brokenness, dysfunction, or even abuse within their families. When they try as adults to have a relationship with their parents, they are met with criticism, rejection, or denial of past abuse. In such circumstances, honoring our parents may require a different approach. It may mean seeking healing and reconciliation where possible and within appropriate boundaries; finding ways to honor our parents from afar, such as by refusing to speak ill of them; expressing gratitude for the good things we received; and remembering them on their birthdays.

Even those who feel their parents do not deserve respect are called to honor them in whatever way they can as unto God, because without them they would not be alive and in the world today. Whether we had great parents who loved us, prepared us for life, and taught us the ways of the kingdom of God, or came from dysfunctional families, we all are to honor our parents the best we can by serving and assisting them.

In addition to addressing our biological parents, the concept of this commandment can be applied to honoring spiritual mentors, caregivers, and anyone who has played a significant role in nurturing and shaping us. It teaches us to recognize and appreciate the investments others have made in our lives.

As we navigate the complexities of family relationships and personal histories, we should seek wisdom from God on how to honor our parents. By keeping the mitzvah to honor one's father and mother (Exod. 20:12), which is the first commandment with a promise (Eph. 6:2), we honor God and build a moral foundation in the earth.

THE PROHIBITION AGAINST MURDER

You shall not murder.
—Exodus 20:13

This mitzvah prohibits the wrongful killing of innocent people, marking the great value God places on the lives of those created in His image. Jewish law distinguishes between acts of violence that occur in the context of capital punishment, war, or self-defense and the deliberate taking of an innocent life. This signifies that murder is not merely a physical act but involves malicious intent.

Murder is not just the taking of someone's life but reflects the attitudes and ambitions of the heart. The account of Cain and Abel in Genesis 4, the first murder we read about in Scripture, serves as a poignant illustration of this.

Cain murdered his brother Abel because he was angry that the Lord accepted Abel's sacrifice but not his. Right before Cain killed his brother, God asked him: "Why are you angry? And why has your countenance fallen? If you do well, will not your countenance be lifted up? And if you do not do well, sin is crouching at the door; and its desire is for you, but you must master it" (Gen. 4:6–7). God was calling Cain to master his anger toward Abel. He was showing Cain that he had a choice to give in to the spirit of hate, anger, and murder, or overcome it. Sadly, Cain yielded to his anger, and as a result he committed the first murder and lived under a curse the rest of his life (Gen. 4:12–16).

Messiah Jesus said Satan was "a murderer from the beginning" (John 8:44), and the apostle John wrote, "Everyone who hates his brother is a murderer" (1 John 3:15). Those who walk in the spirit of murder and hate align themselves with the realm of evil. As followers of Yeshua we are called to walk in love and to overcome. We need to guard our hearts against the spirit of murder, which can include having ill will toward someone, wanting to see them hurt, or rejoicing in their suffering. Speaking for God, Moses said to Israel, "I have set before you life and death, the blessing and the curse. So choose life in order that you may live" (Deut. 30:19). We must resist hate, which is rooted in the spirit of murder, and by the act of our will choose to love.

Proverbs 4:23 admonishes us to watch over our hearts "with all diligence, for from it flow the springs of life." God is life, and murder in its essence is the antithesis of life.

One powerful way we can choose death over life is through the words we say. Our speech can do more harm to someone than robbing them. Stolen money can be repaid, but the harm done by speech cannot easily be repaired. Judaism teaches that the tongue is so dangerous it must be kept under guard by two protective walls, the lips and teeth, to prevent its misuse.[6] James 3:8–10 tells us we can choose to speak blessings or curses, meaning our words have the potential to produce life or death in others. Therefore, we are called to exercise caution and restraint in our speech, making sure our words reflect the life-giving power of God's Spirit rather than the spirit of destruction.

The mitzvah prohibiting murder (Exod. 20:13) reminds us to watch the attitudes and intentions of our hearts and cultivate a spirit of love, compassion, and forgiveness. In doing this, we recognize the sanctity of human life and show honor and holy reverence to our Creator.

THE PROHIBITION AGAINST ADULTERY

You shall not commit adultery.
—Exodus 20:14

At its core this commandment safeguards God's design for the sacred covenant of marriage. By establishing clear boundaries around sexual activity, this law highlights the immense value God places on matrimony and the holiness of the union between husband and wife. The prohibition against adultery also defends the institution of the family against societal degradation. The foundation of stable societies are strong families in which children are raised by a loving father and mother. Divorce destroys this foundation, and infidelity is one of the leading causes of divorce.

Furthermore, this mitzvah underscores the importance of sexual purity and self-discipline, demanding that individuals govern their passions and desires within the parameters of God's order. One of the areas that separates human beings made in the image of God from the rest of the animal kingdom is that we are called to rule over our carnal natures.

Some Hasidic Orthodox Jews wear a belt at waist level called a gartel (Yiddish for *belt*), illustrating that the upper body of the heart and mind must rule over our base instincts. We are not like animals, which are ruled by their natural urges. Sex as God ordained it takes place between a husband and wife in fulfillment of their marriage covenant. All other forms of sex are unholy according to the Torah, and the people of Israel were not to tolerate either a promiscuous man or a promiscuous woman in their midst.

The English word *adultery* comes from the Latin term *adulterate*, which means to contaminate, pollute, or make impure. Sex outside the boundaries of marriage contaminates us before God, and it contaminates marriages, often leading to divorce. This is why Proverbs 6:32 warns that those who commit adultery destroy themselves.

This law also reminds us that keeping ourselves sexually pure is fundamental to our spiritual well-being. During the Sermon on the Mount, Yeshua said, "Everyone who looks at a woman with lust for her has already committed adultery with her in his heart" (Matt. 5:28). By equating having lustful thoughts with the act of adultery, Messiah extended the prohibition against adultery to the realm of the heart, highlighting the need for integrity not only in our actions but also in our attitudes, intentions, and thought life.

In his letter to the Corinthians the apostle Paul admonishes believers to flee from sexual immorality and honor their bodies as temples of the Holy Spirit. He said, "Every other sin that a man commits is outside the body, but the immoral man sins against his own body. Or do you not know that your body is a temple of the Holy Spirit who is in you, whom you have from God, and that you are not your own? For you have been bought with a price: therefore glorify God in your body" (1 Cor. 6:18–20). In this Paul exhorts us to embrace self-control because sexual sin not only defiles the body but also deeply grieves the Spirit of God.

Additionally, prophetically, just as marital infidelity symbolizes a breach of trust and intimacy, so does spiritual adultery signify a betrayal of our covenant with God. We see this for example in the Book of Hosea, where God uses Hosea's wayward wife as a symbol of Israel's unfaithfulness to Him. We can't claim to love our Maker and then seek fulfillment in the pleasures of the world. James 4:4 warns that "friendship with the world is hostility toward God."

The commandment against adultery (Exod. 20:14) brings clarity to a world shrouded in ethical compromise. As custodians of God's moral law and ambassadors of His kingdom we must uphold the sanctity of marriage and remain steadfast in our commitment to sexual purity, honoring God with our bodies. Adultery not only results in spiritual death but also causes the destruction of families. Let's keep our covenant with God and with those to whom we have said "I do."

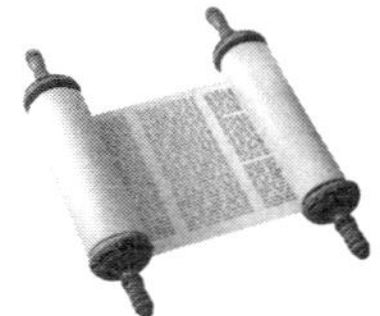

THE PROHIBITION AGAINST THEFT

You shall not steal.
—Exodus 20:15

Though expressed in the context of property rights, this law serves as a moral imperative to behave honestly and fairly in all dealings. The prohibition against stealing reflects a commitment to upholding justice, integrity, and respect for others. By obeying this commandment, we honor the inherent worth and dignity of every person.

Stealing not only violates legal statutes but also breaches fundamental moral principles we all recognize. Whether or not a person believes in God, theft evokes a universal sense of moral outrage, indicating that everyone recognizes the injustice of gaining at someone else's expense. Moreover, stealing signifies a betrayal of the commandment in Leviticus 19:18 to "love your neighbor as yourself," which is echoed in Yeshua's teaching (Mark 12:31). We respect others' property because we respect that God created the person who owns it. When we steal, we commit an offense not only against the one we stole from but against the God who made him.

Exodus 22:4 builds on this commandment by requiring those found guilty of theft to pay double. This serves as both a deterrent and a way of restoring what was stolen. It also compels the perpetrator to confront the consequences of his actions. This reminds me of a movie I saw in which a boy had a special ability to cause the perpetrator of a crime to feel the suffering he had caused his victims. In one scene, a group of sports hunters shot a deer just for fun. The main character forced the killer hunter to place his hands on the head of the deer and experience the pain of the deer as it was dying. Needless to say, the perpetrator had a rude spiritual awakening.

Some may say, "My employer is making so much money it won't hurt him or the company if I misuse my company credit card, take office supplies, or even steal cash." But the Ten Commandments begin with the solemn declaration, "I am the LORD your God" (Exod. 20:2), highlighting that we avoid stealing out of reverence for God. Jewish law actually extends this precept to include not stealing from our employers by fudging our work hours, taking extended coffee breaks, and doing personal internet searches or texting friends while on the clock. To honor this mitzvah prohibiting stealing (Exod. 20:15) is to embrace a lifestyle of integrity, where we discard the excuses and rationalizations and choose instead to obey our Maker and align our actions with His Word.

TO NOT BEAR FALSE WITNESS

You shall not bear false witness against your neighbor.
—Exodus 20:16

In its original context this commandment specifically pertained to testimonies given in legal settings. Bearing false witness was such a violation of God's moral character and a hindrance to the administration of true justice that severe consequences were prescribed for this offense. Deuteronomy 19:18–19 says, "If the witness is a false witness and he has accused his brother falsely, then you shall do to him just as he had intended to do to his brother. Thus you shall purge the evil from among you." The principle of retributive justice spelled out in this passage reveals how much God abhors falsehood, especially when it harms another.

The act of bearing false witness encompasses not only outright perjury but also subtler forms of deception and slander that tarnish people's reputations and dignity. Speaking evil of another is called *lashon hara* in Hebrew. This is considered one of the most serious sins one can commit and has caused numerous tragedies for the Jewish people according to Rabbinic Judaism.[7] Spreading malicious rumors, engaging in gossip, and slanting narratives are grievous to the Holy Spirit. Some who call themselves children of God habitually tell mistruths tainted by their own jealousy, and they don't even realize their words proceed from their lying hearts and a corrupt spirit.

Bearing false witness, slandering, and gossiping are evil acts that defile the one who commits them. Those who engage in this behavior not only release a spirit of death and a curse upon the ones they slander; they also bring a curse and spiritual alienation from God upon themselves.

For followers of The Way, the prohibition against bearing false witness (Exod. 20:16) challenges us to guard our mouths and in so doing reflect God's integrity and goodness.

TO NOT COVET

You shall not covet your neighbor's house; you shall not covet your neighbor's wife or...anything that belongs to your neighbor.
—Exodus 20:17

This commandment constitutes more than an injunction against envy. It is a moral principle that addresses the nature of desire and contentment within the human heart.

By definition, coveting is longing for that which belongs to another. It manifests as an unhealthy fixation on material possessions, relationships, or achievements that are perceived to be lacking in one's own life. To use a lighthearted example, say you give some children each a piece of candy but one decides he doesn't have enough and wants more, so he forcibly takes another child's candy. The result is that one child is now crying and upset, the others are unsettled, and the "thief" eats too much candy and gets sick to his stomach. Nobody wins. So this commandment identifies and seeks to forestall the corrosive effects of envy, reminding individuals of the inherent dangers posed by unchecked desires.

The twelfth-century Torah scholar Rabbi Ibn Ezra provides commentary on this law and addresses the difficulty of not desiring things that are appealing. In his explanation he employs a parable in which a sensible peasant refrains from coveting a princess because he recognizes the impossibility of such a desire. A wise person, then, understands the futility of coveting what is prohibited or unattainable. Instead, we trust in God's providence and provision for us.

Our heavenly Father wants us to bless and thank Him for where we are and what we already have. It is sometimes good to desire more—spiritually, emotionally, relationally, or financially. But when our desire for more is not restrained by godly morals and tempered with wisdom, we end up destroying ourselves and the world around us.

Coveting is also about our *internal thoughts and desires.* It is worth pointing out that the precept against coveting (which is the last of the Ten Commandments) can be broken not just by our physical actions but by engaging in wrong thoughts. Stealing, which we covered in a previous law, involves doing something in the physical realm, but coveting happens in the heart.

To desire things in life is natural, but to obsess over anything that is not ours produces torment and shows we lack a divine perspective. Someone once said that a rich man is not someone who can buy anything he wants but one who feels blessed with what he has. I have met people with mediocre jobs and mediocre finances, yet they have a regalness about them because of their satisfaction with who they are. On the other side of the coin, there are wealthy people who are miserable despite having billions of dollars.

Gaining possession of what we covet does not make us happier. Paul told Timothy, "If we have food and covering, with these we shall be content" (1 Tim. 6:8). The author of Hebrews instructs God's children to learn how to be "content with what you have" (Heb. 13:5). Again, it is natural to want good things, but the purpose of this commandment is to keep us from desiring things in a way that defiles us and removes God from the throne of our affections.

I once had a dream in which I was trying to find my way home, and I took a path that led to a house where a party was being held. At this house was the most ostentatious, extravagant, over-the-top wealth I had ever seen. Everything was the absolute best money could buy. At the back of the home there was a pool surrounded by an exquisite Italian marble deck. As I approached it, I saw people lying all around the deck, utterly wasted, as if they were strung out on drugs. Despite their wealth and possessions—the finest money could buy—the people living in such gluttonous opulence were empty, hollow shells with hearts vacant of peace or fulfillment.

Recently while in Israel, I talked with an American woman who had moved to Israel some years before. She told me that her kids are so much better there than they were in the United States, where they constantly *wanted things*. Their affections kept reaching for the next, newest thing, but none of it satisfied them. Desires are endless, and the flesh can never ultimately be satisfied.

Let's use the Spirit's discernment to separate what God really desires for us from unholy desires. James said, "But each one is tempted when he is *carried away* and enticed by his own lust. Then when lust has conceived, it gives birth to sin; and when sin is accomplished, it brings forth death. Do not be deceived, my beloved brethren. Every good thing given and every perfect gift is from above, coming down from the Father of lights" (Jas. 1:14–17, emphasis added).

In this passage we see the difference between receiving God's gifts and coveting, which leads to sin. Coveting is one reason so many are suffering the agony of financial debt. People purchase on credit what is beyond their means to own. James calls what God offers "a perfect gift"—it does not bring indebtedness and anxiety along with it.

We need to learn to be content with our possessions and circumstances while at the same time pressing into all our God has for us. Paul said he was always pressing "on toward the goal for the prize of the upward call of God in Christ Jesus" (Phil. 3:14). Yet he also said in Philippians 4:11–12: "I have learned to be content in whatever circumstances I am. I know how to get along with humble means, and I also know how to live in prosperity; in any and every circumstance I have learned the secret of being filled and going hungry, both of having abundance and suffering need."

For six of our first ten years of marriage, my wife, Cynthia, and I lived in a mobile home. Yet Cynthia never complained. Instead, she would look out the window at the vacant lot next to our mobile home and talk about how beautiful the scenery was. Don't let coveting rob you of peace or distract you by drawing your eyes to that which is not yet yours. May the precept against coveting (Exod. 20:17) stir you to find peace in Messiah today. Trust that as you give Him your best, He will give you His best.

COMMANDMENT DEALING WITH HOW GOD'S PRIESTS SHOULD DRESS

And you shall not go up by steps to My altar, so that your nakedness will not be exposed on it.
—Exodus 20:26

This commandment instructed priests not to ascend to the altar by stair steps to prevent their nakedness from being exposed to those standing below them. This was a practical measure to maintain the dignity and sanctity of the priestly service and ensured that no indecency occurred during worship. By requiring the priests to ascend by a ramp rather than steps so those below could not look up their robes, God also reveals and communicates the importance of modesty and reverence in approaching Him.

When it was given, this mitzvah was part of the broader framework of regulations governing the Tabernacle and its services. The Tabernacle was the central place of worship for the Israelites, where they offered sacrifices and sought God's presence. As such, it was essential that all aspects of worship, including the attire and conduct of the priests, reflect the holiness of God and uphold the purity of the sacred space.

The priests were instructed to dress in garments of "glory and beauty," which reflect God's nature and the holiness of the priests' calling (Exod. 28:2). God embodies perfect beauty. We can be attractive and dress beautifully without drawing people to our flesh. We can dress well without dressing sensuously.

All believers now belong to a royal priesthood (1 Pet. 2:9) and are called to attire ourselves in a manner that honors God and reflects His glory. First Timothy 2:9 says, "Likewise, I want women to adorn themselves with proper clothing, modestly and discreetly, not with braided hair and gold or pearls or costly garments." Our clothing should be chosen to glorify God, not to arouse a sexual response. Our bodies are temples of the Holy Spirit (1 Cor. 6:19).

In Israel, Orthodox Jewish women wear skirts that fall below their knees. These Orthodox women are just as attractive, if not more so, than those who flaunt themselves. More flesh is not better. In countries where people can walk around nude, nakedness loses its appeal. God's path of modesty is more satisfying and healthy in the long run in every way.

Personally, there came a time when I started being mindful of how I buttoned my shirts because I realized that having too many buttons undone was drawing people to my flesh and not as modest as I thought suitable for me as God's servant. Practically speaking, men and women should not wear clothes so tight that nothing is left to the imagination. A woman should not show inappropriate cleavage or wear short skirts. Men as well need to apply this same principle to their clothing selections. Our salvation does not depend on what we wear, but again, we honor our Maker when we choose attire that does not draw people to our flesh. Are our clothing selections meant to impress others and draw them to our flesh, or do we dress with the intent to glorify God?

Modesty encompasses being mindful of how we present ourselves in various settings, including worship. Just as the priests were careful to avoid any potential exposure of their nakedness before the altar, we are called to approach God and stand before His people with reverence. We must not conform to the standards of the world but be transformed by the renewing of our minds (Rom. 12:2).

Just because the world dresses or acts in a certain way doesn't mean God's people should follow suit. While society may promote sensuality and immodesty, believers are called to set ourselves apart and uphold a higher standard of purity. This often requires resisting fashion trends and instead buying clothes that honor God. We can dress attractively without crossing the line into sensuality. We must remember that as God's sons and daughters, we stand before Him in Yeshua at the altar every day. May the commandment addressing how God's priests should dress (Exod. 20:26) inspire us to adorn ourselves in a way that displays His beauty and holiness.

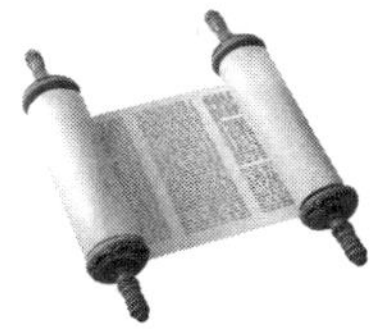

THE PROHIBITION AGAINST MEN SEDUCING WOMEN

If a man seduces a virgin who is not engaged, and lies with her, he must pay a dowry for her to be his wife.
—Exodus 22:16

This commandment addresses seduction and its consequences. Given to Israel approximately 3,500 years ago, this law may seem antiquated and irrelevant to contemporary society, yet it contains profound spiritual applications that transcend time and culture.

In its original context this precept preserved the rights and dignity of women, particularly unmarried virgins. In ancient Near Eastern cultures a woman's virginity was highly valued, and any violation of it had serious implications for her social standing and future marriage prospects. By requiring the seducer to take responsibility for his actions and marry the woman he seduced, God protected women from exploitation and dishonor.

Then and now, this commandment serves as a warning to men regarding the sanctity of sexual relations. In many societies, including ancient Israel, sexual conquests were often seen as emblematic of masculinity and virility. Similarly, chasing women, picking up girls, and so forth are viewed as fun and acceptable behaviors by many nonbelievers today.

However, God's perspective on sex is radically different. In His eyes, sexual intimacy is a sacred gift to be enjoyed in the context of holy matrimony. Sexual sin is a serious matter, and its consequences go beyond the immediate physical act. When a man engages in intimate relations with a woman, he does not merely indulge in physical pleasure. In the Creator's eyes, he enters into a covenantal relationship with her. Again, according to biblical law, sexual relations create a bond between a man and woman that is equivalent to marriage, regardless of whether a formal ceremony has taken place.

This is why it is imperative for believers to bring their sexual conduct under God's authority. The apostle Paul calls us in 2 Timothy 2:22 to "flee from youthful lusts and pursue righteousness, faith, love and peace." This, of course, means that we as God's people are to honor His design for sexuality and refrain from actions that dishonor Him and harm others.

This command obligating a man who seduces a virgin who is not engaged to marry her (Exod. 22:16) challenges prevailing standards in contemporary society that allow casual and indiscriminate sexual behavior. We are called to resist the temptations of the flesh and live pleasing unto God as those who are holy and chosen.

THE PROHIBITION AGAINST WITCHCRAFT

You shall not allow a sorceress to live.
—Exodus 22:18

The law forbidding witchcraft, as outlined in Exodus 22:18 and reiterated in Leviticus 19:31, reflects God's unequivocal stance against practices that involve mediums, spiritists, or sorcerers. In ancient Israel, witchcraft and sorcery were serious offenses punishable by death. While the cultural context of these prohibitions may seem distant and unfamiliar to some modern readers, the underlying spiritual principles remain relevant and applicable today.

The fact is that in contemporary society there is a growing fascination with supernatural phenomena, occult practices, witchcraft, and unbiblical methods of seeking to contact other realms. The commandments prohibiting witchcraft warn us against the ever-present dangers of spiritual deception and idolatry. Many people are drawn to horoscopes, tarot card readings, and channeling in search of spiritual guidance and enlightenment.

Additionally, some believers in Jesus become addicted to receiving words of personal prophecy, attending meeting after meeting in search of the next word for their lives. This can become a form of witchcraft or an unholy, pseudo-Christian version of fortune-telling.

Others from certain traditions pray to saints or hold on to superstitions. When I was in Peru, I visited a museum displaying various statues of Jesus that people prayed to based on their needs. If they needed a financial blessing, they prayed to one statue; for other needs, they prayed to another, mixing their Judeo-Christian beliefs with elements of folk religions. Many who identify as Christians but who are not grounded in the Word and sound doctrine inadvertently mix New Age beliefs into their worldview and perception of reality. Even occultic forms of *Jewish* mysticism are seeing a resurgence in popularity.

God's Word explicitly prohibits His people from engaging in such activities. The reason is twofold. First, these practices are often rooted in demonic deception and manipulation, and second, they undermine the authority and sufficiency of God's Word and Spirit. Believers are called to seek guidance and wisdom from Adonai alone, trusting in His provision to guide them.

In today's pluralistic society people tend to blend elements of different religious traditions and spiritual practices to create their own personalized, eclectic spirituality. However, God's Word sternly forbids mixing the holy with the profane. Paul asked rhetorically, "What fellowship has light with darkness? Or what harmony has Christ with Belial?" (2 Cor. 6:14–15). We are called to maintain a genuine and undefiled faith in Yeshua without entertaining compromise with worldly ideologies and practices.

The prohibition against witchcraft (Exod. 22:18) serves as a timeless reminder of God's holiness and sovereignty over all spiritual powers and principalities. We are called to reject the deceptive allure of occult practices and New Age spirituality, instead trusting in Yahweh alone for guidance, protection, and provision.

TO NOT CURSE GOD AND LEADERS

You shall not curse God, nor curse a ruler of your people.
—Exodus 22:28

The commandment against cursing God and leaders underscores the importance of reverencing, respecting, and submitting to both divine and earthly authorities, thus honoring the order established by HaShem. In its original context, cursing God or a ruler was regarded as a serious transgression deserving of severe consequences. We see this in the Book of Numbers:

> Miriam and Aaron spoke against Moses….Then the Lord came down in a pillar of cloud and stood at the doorway of the tent, and He called Aaron and Miriam. When they had both come forward, He said…"Why then were you not afraid to speak against My servant, against Moses?" So the anger of the Lord burned against them and He departed. But when the cloud had withdrawn from over the tent, behold, Miriam was leprous, as white as snow. As Aaron turned toward Miriam, behold, she was leprous.
>
> —Numbers 12:1, 5–6, 8–10

Then and now, the prohibition in Exodus 22:8 reinforces the sanctity of God's name and cultivates an environment of respect and order within the community. For followers of Yeshua, why we shouldn't curse God is self-evident, but what escapes many is the seriousness of cursing leaders. Often today God's people are sensitive to sin but not to authority. They fail to realize that cursing leaders actually reveals a disrespect and lack of reverence for God. In Romans 13 the apostle Paul affirms the divine origin of all authority, declaring that "there is no authority except from God, and those which exist are established by God" (v. 1).

I know many people may think, "But that politician is corrupt"; "That president is immoral"; or, "That judge is a liberal and makes ungodly rulings." Some rightly wonder, "What about leaders like Hitler and Mussolini, who killed millions of people?" Yes, there are times to react to unjust leadership, but the problem in our culture is that respect for authority and its institutions has collapsed. When there is no respect for authority and its institutions, chaos ensues.

Again, authority brings God's order. This is why the Torah says we shall not curse a judge (Exod. 22:28, TLB). Despite the imperfections of human leaders, their authority is ultimately delegated by God for the purpose of maintaining peace and justice in society. God's people are called to respect positions of authority out of devotion to Him, regardless of the personal qualities or actions of individual leaders.

This commandment reminds us of Adon Olam's (the Master of the Universe's) supremacy. Cursing God not only demonstrates a lack of reverence for His divine authority but reflects a rebellious attitude toward His sovereignty. While it may be tempting to carelessly criticize or condemn leaders we perceive as corrupt or unjust, we must also uphold the truth that authority is established by the Most High. This does not mean turning a blind eye to injustice or condoning wrongdoing, but rather seeking to address concerns with a right attitude through appropriate channels and means, in accordance with biblical principles.

Moreover, the precept against cursing God and leaders (Exod. 22:28) serves as a countercultural reminder of the importance of upholding structure in society. In a culture where skepticism and cynicism toward authority are prevalent, we as believers are called to demonstrate a different way of living, characterized by respect for divinely established positions of leadership. In so doing, we promote God's ordained order in the earth.

TO NOT DELAY THE OFFERING FROM ONE'S HARVEST AND VINTAGE

You shall not delay the offering from your harvest and your vintage.
—Exodus 22:29

This instruction, given in the context of Old Testament agricultural practices and the religious customs of ancient Israel, was meant to ensure the Israelites honored God with the firstfruits of their produce without delay. It also spoke to the principle of giving back to God from the abundance He had provided, acknowledging His provision and sovereignty over their lives.

This commandment identifies and points out that honoring our Creator with our substance is an important aspect of the way we relate to Him. Just as the Israelites were instructed to offer the firstfruits of their harvests to God, those of us who have been purchased by Yeshua's blood are called to present tithes and offerings to the Lord as an expression of our gratitude, trust, and obedience.

Firstfruits offerings are symbolically significant in the Bible, representing the best and choicest portion of possessions offered to God as an act of worship. This command specifies that we should present our offerings *without delay.*

Procrastination can hinder our relationship with God and impede His blessings in our lives. I have found that when God speaks to me about presenting an offering to Him, the time to do it is immediately while I have the faith and grace to do it.

When I don't obey immediately, I begin to doubt and question the Holy Spirit's prompting. At times when I have not obeyed, I have grieved, wondering what blessing I missed from not practicing instant obedience.

When we withhold or delay our offerings to God, we not only disobey His commands but also miss out on the blessings that come from timely obedience. The prohibition against delaying one's offering (Exod. 22:29) calls us to put God's interests first, before ours and before any other purpose.

As we present our offerings to the Lord with gratitude and trust, we honor Him and invite His favor and provision into our lives.

TO NOT FOLLOW AN EVIL MAJORITY

You shall not follow the masses in doing evil, nor
shall you testify in a dispute so as to turn aside
after a multitude in order to pervert justice.
—Exodus 23:2

This mitzvah calls us to resist social pressures to compromise our integrity for the sake of conformity. In its original context, this precept guarded the principles of justice and righteousness within the community of Israel by commanding individuals to not be swayed by the prevailing attitudes, opinions, or actions of the majority, if the majority was not aligned with Yahweh and His Word.

Some commentators believe this commandment was specifically directed at judges, warning them to execute justice impartially and not be swayed by the pressure of others. Today, partisan politics has weaponized the judicial system so that true justice does not always prevail. Furthermore, the secular, liberal masses are influencing leaders, judges, and institutions to make decisions that pervert God's standards of holiness and righteousness in the earth.

From a broader spiritual perspective, this commandment cautions us against the dangers of moral relativism and of departing from our faith and values. In an age in which cultural standards often conflict with biblical principles—on subjects such as abortion, premarital sex, and the LGBTQ agenda, to name just a few—we are called to resist temptations to conform to the patterns of this age. Popular or widely accepted norms are not necessarily right in God's eyes. As followers of The Way, we are called to be salt and light in the world, standing firm in our convictions and reflecting the righteousness of God's kingdom and a biblical worldview.

Again, this precept warns us against perverting justice by yielding to the influence of the majority. Examples abound throughout history of individuals who courageously stood against evil in their times, people like German theologian Dietrich Bonhoeffer, who bravely resisted the Nazi regime and lost his life as a result. In Scripture, Daniel and his friends refused to bow down to the idol of Nebuchadnezzar, and Yeshua refused to compromise the message of the gospel to save His life.

In Acts 5:29 Peter and the other apostles declared, "We must obey God rather than men," when authorities confronted them demanding they stop preaching in Yeshua's name. Moral courage often means facing the headwinds of prevailing opinion.

The command against following an evil majority (Exod. 23:2) reminds us to hold firm to our convictions and resist the pressures to conform for the sake of man's approval, even when it costs us.

TO TREAT ANIMALS WITH COMPASSION

If you see the donkey of one who hates you lying helpless under its load, you shall refrain from leaving it to him, you shall surely release it with him.
—Exodus 23:5

The commandment spelled out in Exodus 23:5 and reiterated in Deuteronomy 22:4 compels us to treat animals with kindness, calling attention to our responsibility to steward God's creation with care and reflect His love and mercy to all living beings.

The specific scenario described in Exodus 23:5 involves encountering the donkey of someone who harbors hostility toward us lying helpless under its pack. Despite any personal animosity that may exist between the two parties, the commandment instructs them not to ignore the plight of the animal but to intervene to relieve its suffering. To put it simply, the Torah requires us to alleviate the pain of animals: "A righteous man has regard for the life of his animal" (Prov. 12:10).

This commandment is exemplified in the life of Francis of Assisi, a renowned Christian mystic considered the patron saint of animals. The founder of the Franciscan religious order within Catholicism, Francis was famously compassionate toward all living beings, especially animals, and advocated for their protection and well-being. He referred to animals as his brothers and sisters and is said to have convinced a wolf to stop its attacks on the people and livestock of the Italian town of Gubbio in exchange for the townspeople agreeing to feed it.[8]

During the days of Noah, after the floodwaters subsided and the ark landed on the mountain Ararat, God said to Noah: "Now behold, I Myself do establish My covenant with you...and with every living creature that is with you, the birds, the cattle, and every beast of the earth with you; of all that comes out of the ark, even every beast of the earth....This is the sign of the covenant which I am making between Me and you and every living creature that is with you, for all successive generations" (Gen. 9:9–10, 12). Note that God's covenant was not only with Noah but with "every living creature" with him.

This mitzvah challenging us to treat animals with compassion (Exod. 23:5) sensitizes us to the reality that animals are valuable and precious to the God who created them and not simply commodities to be callously used.

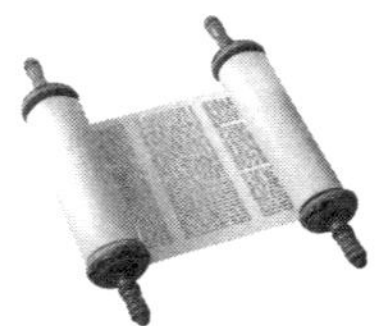

TO LET THE LAND REST ON THE SEVENTH YEAR

> You shall sow your land for six years and gather in its yield, but on the seventh year you shall let it rest and lie fallow, so that the needy of your people may eat; and whatever they leave the beast of the field may eat. You are to do the same with your vineyard and your olive grove.
> —Exodus 23:10–11

The Israelites were to cultivate their land for six years, but in the seventh year, known as the Shemitah, they were to let it lie fallow. During this Sabbath year, the needy among the people were permitted to eat from the produce of the land, and whatever remained was available to the beasts of the field. Heeding the Shemitah was an act of faith that God would supply and a recognition of His sovereignty over the earth. By obeying this commandment, the Israelites demonstrated trust in His ability to meet all their needs, even when they ceased their agricultural efforts for an entire year.

I imagine this didn't seem to make sense to ancient Israel. It's likely many wondered, "How can we be prosperous if we don't till the land for a full year? Will we have enough harvest for the future?" But the rabbis teach that obeying God when we don't understand reflects the highest form of devotion and love for Him.

The prophetic application of the Shemitah is twofold. First, it teaches us the importance of exercising faith in response to

God's precepts, even when His commands may not make sense to our natural minds. In obeying this mitzvah, the Israelites demonstrated their trust in God, who declared in Isaiah 55:9, "For as the heavens are higher than the earth, so are My ways higher than your ways and My thoughts than your thoughts."

Just as it took faith for the people of Israel to stop cultivating their land during the Sabbath year, trusting that God would provide, so we must trust God and obey Him during times when His direction doesn't make sense to us. I can recount numerous examples from my own life when I obeyed God though it didn't make logical sense and as a result He orchestrated great blessings in a short period of time, accomplishing what would not have been possible in a lifetime of human effort. Miracles can happen when we rest in faith rather than striving ceaselessly in our own strength, as this law concerning the Shemitah points to.

I recall the year I took off of work just to sit before the Lord. After about nine months I wondered, "Is this responsible?" I prayed, "God, if You want me to just keep doing nothing but waiting on You, let there be an unexpected check in my mailbox today." When I went to my mailbox, there was a substantial check from someone I had never met. God was confirming my decision to honor Him with a Shemitah year. By resting from our labors periodically by the direction of the Holy Spirit, we affirm that we trust God to supply our needs and recognize that His favor is the source of our provision. It is important to work, but it is also important to rest and, above all else, obey Him.

Second, the Shemitah reminds us of God's creative power and authority over all. He created the world in six days and rested on the seventh. By resting in the seventh year, the Israelites emulated the Creator and affirmed His role as the Master of the Universe and sustainer of all life.

As the Israelites demonstrated faith in God's ability to meet their needs even while they let the land rest in the seventh year (Exod. 23:10–11), so too we must trust in God's transcending character by obeying His Word and Spirit, even when we can't comprehend His ways.

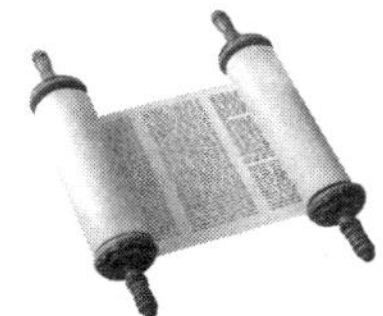

TO NOT BOIL A YOUNG GOAT IN ITS MOTHER'S MILK

You are not to boil a young goat in the milk of its mother.
—Exodus 23:19

This prohibition may initially appear enigmatic, but upon closer examination it underscores God's concern for the sanctity of life and the need to treat all creatures with compassion and respect. From the words of this mitzvah the rabbis extrapolated a complex set of dietary laws, which to this day prohibit observant Orthodox Jews from eating foods containing milk and meat together. This rabbinic prohibition against eating dairy and meat products together is part of the laws known as *kashrut*, or keeping kosher.

While the literal interpretation of boiling a young goat in its mother's milk may come across as obscure, consider some deeper insights. To boil a young goat in its mother's milk reveals a disregard not only for the sanctity of life but also for the important relationships animals have with their offspring. Furthermore, this law recognizes the interconnectedness and interdependence of all living creatures. Animals are able to feel and sense more than we realize. Consider the insensitivity of some dog owners who chain their pets outside and let them bark all day with the sun beating down. Often they don't provide them enough water, food, or exercise, or show them affection. Their behavior contradicts the principle in this verse and demonstrates a lack of sensitivity to the Creator.

The prohibition against boiling a young goat in its mother's milk (Exod. 23:19) challenges us, as stewards of God's creation, to see and recognize the intrinsic dignity of all creatures. This may take various forms, such as respecting the relationship between a mother animal and her child, showing affection to pets, or providing plants or livestock with proper water, food, shelter, and care. In so doing, we recognize God's relationship with His creation and align our hearts with His empathy for all living things.

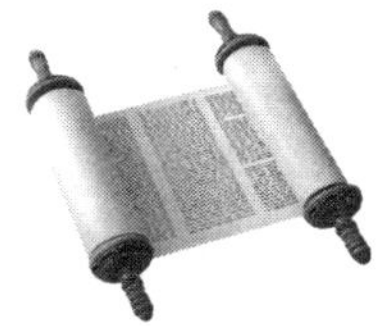

TO NOT MAKE ANY COVENANT WITH A HEATHEN NATION

You shall make no covenant with them or with their gods. They shall not live in your land, because they will make you sin against Me; for if you serve their gods, it will surely be a snare to you.
—Exodus 23:32–33

This command is rooted in the understanding that any covenant with a heathen nation or its gods inevitably leads to idolatry and spiritual compromise. In ancient Israel, covenanting with heathen nations meant entering into political alliances, trade partnerships, or intermarriages. These agreements were not merely political or economic; they often involved religious syncretism, where the gods of the heathen nations were acknowledged or even worshipped. God prohibited such covenants to prevent His people from being led astray by foreign gods and practices, which would corrupt their allegiance to Him.

The warning of the law is clear: "They shall not live in your land, because they will make you sin against Me; for if you serve their gods, it will surely be a snare to you" (Exod. 23:33). The presence of the gods of the heathen nations would prove a constant temptation and lead to Israel's downfall. By avoiding making covenants with these nations, Israel would remain a holy and distinct people, set apart to worship the one true Creator, Yahweh, the Blessed One.

For believers in Yeshua today, this commandment offers

significant lessons. The principle of not making covenants with heathen nations can be understood as a call to avoid forming close alliances with people, groups, or institutions that could lead us away from God. It also cautions us about coming into binding agreements with any person or entity whose behavior and beliefs contradict biblical values.

Further application of this principle can take various forms. For instance, we are to avoid business partnerships that may erode our ethical standards, such as purchasing stock in companies whose agenda is unbiblical. This law should also cause us to consider where we are sending our children to be educated. We are increasingly seeing how secular universities and some public schools are infecting our children with unbiblical worldviews and advocating unholy lifestyles that lead them away from God and His truth.

Prophetically, many of God's people are violating this commandment by what they are allowing into their homes via the mediums of the internet, TV, and radio. Notice Exodus 23:33 says, "They shall not live in your land." It is not the internet, TV, or radio that is the evil; it is what we have allowed into our lives through them.

By refraining from ill-advised partnerships and relationships, Israel had to rely solely on God for its security and provision. May the precept to make no covenant with a heathen nation (Exod. 23:32–33) move us to put our faith in God alone, believing that He will bless us as we refuse any agreement that may lead to compromise in our relationship with Him.

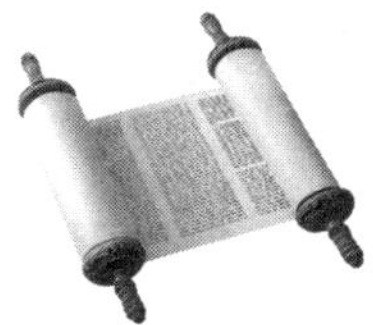

TO BUILD A SANCTUARY FOR GOD

Let them construct a sanctuary for Me,
that I may dwell among them.
—Exodus 25:8

This command to Israel to build a sanctuary for the Lord reveals God's desire to be in relationship with His people. The Israelites did indeed erect a sanctuary called the Tabernacle, known in Hebrew as the Mishkan. God's presence dwelled among them there, manifesting above it as a cloud of glory by day and a pillar of fire by night for the forty years they were in the wilderness traveling to the Promised Land.

Once Israel entered the Promised Land, they converted the portable Tabernacle into a permanent structure in Jerusalem called the Temple. The Temple was built under the reign of King Solomon on Mount Moriah, where Abraham bound Isaac on an altar to sacrifice him (Gen. 22:1–2) and where an angel of the Lord appeared to Solomon's father, David (2 Chron. 3:1).

Although the Romans destroyed the Temple in AD 70, its prophetic significance is still immensely meaningful today. We have become the temple of the Holy Spirit (1 Cor. 6:19). As the ancient Temple was holy, so we must be holy, unique, different, set apart, and cut out of this world unto the Lord, offering ourselves up as living sacrifices to Him (Rom. 12:1). In so doing, we create within us a sanctuary where God's presence dwells.

The construction of the Temple in Jerusalem carries further

symbolic significance because in God's eyes, Jerusalem is the center of the world from which His grace flows to the entire earth.

> Thus says the Lord God, "This is Jerusalem; I have set her at the center of the nations, with lands around her."
>
> —Ezekiel 5:5

Likewise, as Yeshua's disciples we are ambassadors of God's kingdom who carry His presence wherever we go, even to the uttermost parts of the world. Just as the sanctuary in Jerusalem was a beacon of God's presence to the nations, so too we as believers are called to be bearers of light and truth to the entire globe.

Even as Israel was commanded to do the work of "constructing" a sanctuary for Yahweh (Exod. 25:8), as Yeshua's disciples we must do the spiritual work of sanctifying our hearts, creating a sanctuary and dwelling place for the living God to abide within us.

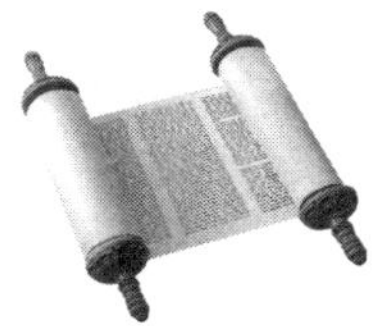

TO MAKE THE LIGHT BURN IN THE LAMPSTAND WITHIN THE TEMPLE CONTINUALLY

You shall charge the sons of Israel, that they bring you clear oil of beaten olives for the light, to make a lamp burn continually.
—Exodus 27:20

This commandment to the sons of Israel called them to provide clear oil to keep the lamps in the Tabernacle, and later the Temple, burning continually. The oil used was produced by the first pressing of the olives, ensuring that it was clear and free of residue. The clarity of this oil speaks to God's purity, and the fact that this oil was produced by the first pressing of the olives symbolizes the Most High's incredible, inconceivable value.

The lamp in the Temple, representing the Spirit of God, was perpetually burning. This conveys the continuous radiance of God's presence in the created world and the lives of His people. Like a flame of fire, the Spirit of the Lord, the Ruach HaKodesh, is always active and moving. In fact, God's personal name, Yahweh, implies that He exists in a state of continuous unfinished action. We see this expressed in Isaiah 6 and Revelation 4, which describe the scene around God's throne. Day and night the angelic beings never cease crying, "Holy, holy, holy." They do this because new emanations of God's holiness and glory are continually bubbling forth. Each time they say "Holy," they are responding to a fresh, new unfolding manifestation of who He is.

There is always more of God to discover, and He desires to draw us into an ever-deepening state of experiencing His presence. But just as the sons of Israel were to supply clear oil so the lamp would burn continually, so we must be intentional about nurturing our relationship with Him. When we begin our days sitting before the Lord, rededicating our lives to Him and asking Him to make us more aware of His Spirit, we are supplying clear oil. When we invite Him to cleanse us of all sin and darkness, we are presenting Him with clear oil. The Spirit is just as alive and active today as He was when the Scriptures were written.

Note that it was the task of "the sons of Israel," not just the priests, to provide the oil for the lamp so it would burn continually. Rabbi Yeshua said, "You are the light of the world. A city set on a hill cannot be hidden....Let your light shine before men in such a way that they may see your good works, and glorify your Father who is in heaven" (Matt. 5:14, 16). We must recognize the importance of being intentional witnesses of the Light—Yeshua—in both word and deed.

The commandment to maintain the oil in the lampstand within the Temple so it burns continually (Exod. 27:20) serves as a powerful reminder to us to be God's light-bearers in the world.

THE COMMAND FOR THE PRIESTS TO WEAR SPECIAL GARMENTS

You shall make holy garments for Aaron your brother, for glory and for beauty....These are the garments which they shall make: a breastpiece and an ephod and a robe and a tunic of checkered work, a turban and a sash, and they shall make holy garments for Aaron your brother and his sons, that he may minister as priest to Me.
—Exodus 28:2, 4

The precept for the priests to wear special garments holds both practical and symbolic significance. While it was originally given to Aaron and his sons for their role as priests in the Tabernacle, it offers timeless application for all God's people.

The garments were designed "for glory and for beauty," reflecting the majesty and splendor of God's essence. David said, "One thing I have asked from the Lord, that I shall seek: That I may dwell in the house of the Lord all the days of my life, *to behold the beauty of the Lord* and to meditate in His temple" (Ps. 27:4, emphasis added). Just as the priests were instructed to dress in garments that reflected God's glory, so too are believers called to live and dress in a manner that reflects God's beauty and honors Him.

Years ago our congregation's worship leader and I attended an event at a large church. One of their worship leaders was wearing pants that were skintight from her ankle to her hips. I asked our worship leader, "Why is she dressed like that?" He said, "That's the way the culture dresses." Rather than drawing attention to the glory of God, her attire detracted from the worship experience and invited a focus on her physical attributes. Her choice of what to wear went against the essence of this commandment.

God wants us to be clothed in the anointing of His holiness. But instead, many believers try to live by the power of the flesh, using their sensual allure, status, or physique to manipulate or influence others. There is nothing wrong with dressing attractively in a godly way and taking care of ourselves to reflect God's excellency, but that should not be our focus. Our aim should be to reflect God's glory and beauty in the earth.

One of the garments for glory and beauty that the high priest wore was a breastplate that contained twelve gemstones representing the twelve tribes of Israel. Just as Aaron the high priest carried the names of the tribes over his heart when he entered the Holy Place, so we are called to carry one another in prayer and intercession continually. This reflects the heart of Jesus, who prayed for the unity and well-being of all His people (John 17).

Even as the high priest's breastplate contained a gem for each one of the twelve tribes, we should carry a burden for the whole body of Messiah. Too often our prayers are consumed only with our own needs. We should intercede for the building of God's kingdom and people worldwide. As Moses carried a burden for all Israel (Exod. 33:12–23), so we should maintain a heart of compassion and intercession for all our holy brothers and sisters in the faith.

As believers we are called to adorn ourselves with the beauty of holiness both physically and spiritually. Let us heed this commandment for the priests to wear special garments (Exod. 28:2, 4) by dressing in a way that glorifies God and sincerely praying for one another.

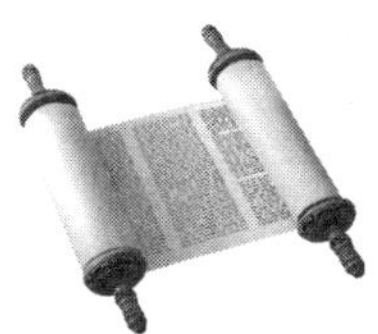

TO BURN INCENSE OF SWEET SPICES UNTO THE LORD EVERY MORNING

Aaron shall burn fragrant incense on it; he shall burn it every morning....There shall be perpetual incense before the LORD throughout your generations.
—EXODUS 30:7–8

THIS COMMANDMENT CALLED God's priests to rise above the flesh and the tiredness they felt when they woke up in the morning to ascend to a place of giving adoration and devotion to Yahweh. Spiritually, the burning of incense represents the offering of prayers and worship to the Holy One. Just as the fragrant incense ascended before the Lord at dawn in the Temple, so believers are called to lift prayers and praise to HaShem at the start of each day.

The "perpetual" burning of incense before the Lord throughout the generations symbolizes the timeless nature of prayer and worship. Just as the incense was to burn continually, so too are believers called to maintain a lifestyle of prayer and worship, offering up praises and petitions to God night and day. In Psalm 141:2 David wrote, "May my prayer be counted as incense before You; the lifting up of my hands as the evening offering." And in Psalm 5:3 he prayed, "In the morning, O LORD, You will hear my voice; in the morning I will order my prayer to You and eagerly watch."

In the New Testament we are exhorted to pray without ceasing, offering up our prayers and supplications with thanksgiving (1 Thess. 5:17; Phil. 4:6). It is our joy and privilege to begin each day with prayer and praise.

Let us heed this precept to burn incense of sweet spices unto the Lord every morning (Exod. 30:7–8) by beginning each day with prayer. Just as the fragrant incense ascended before the Lord in the Tabernacle and Temple as a pleasing aroma, so our prayers rise before Him as a welcome and honoring scent.

TO OFFER NO STRANGE INCENSE ON THE ALTAR

You shall not offer any strange incense on this altar, or burnt offering or meal offering; and you shall not pour out a drink offering on it.
—Exodus 30:9

This precept signifies the reality that we must come to God on His terms, not our own. The specific regulations governing the altar of incense established the principle that our worship must align with God's revealed instruction. Only specific incense could be used, and no other offerings were allowed. This reveals the authority, sanctity, and holiness of God and our need to take care in how we approach Him.

As previously noted, incense in Scripture is symbolic of prayer. The incense was to be made of specific spices and prepared in a very particular way. Furthermore, Israel could not use this sacred incense for personal use. This points to the fact that God is not common, and we must relate to Him as the Holy One, not as "the man upstairs."

David, the king of Israel, declared: "Who may ascend into the hill of the Lord? And who may stand in His holy place? He who has clean hands and a pure heart, who has not lifted up his soul to falsehood and has not sworn deceitfully" (Ps. 24:3–4). God needs to be approached with a humble heart that recognizes He is to be revered. To offer, according to this commandment, "strange incense" is to approach Him on our own terms, with an attitude that is not in proper alignment with Him.

Practically, this mitzvah to offer no strange incense on the altar (Exod. 30:9) warns us about coming to God insincerely. I have seen people, for example, offer prayers designed to impress or manipulate others rather than move God's heart. I have heard numerous petitions where the individual praying seemed to be more focused on those hearing them pray than on God. This is offering up strange incense on the altar. Prayers that are voiced for the sake of gaining people's approval, just to make others feel good, or worse yet, to achieve some personal financial gain are, once again, equivalent to strange incense on the altar.

TO NOT OFFER HONEY ON THE ALTAR

You shall not offer up in smoke any leaven or any honey as an offering by fire to the LORD.
—LEVITICUS 2:11

THE OMISSION OF honey as an offering symbolizes the need to have our physical urges under control. Honey tantalizes and excites the flesh by its sweetness. But "flesh and blood cannot inherit the kingdom of God; nor does the perishable inherit the imperishable" (1 Cor. 15:50). God is only accessed by the spirit. Honey, which inflames the passion of the flesh, is forbidden.

Sometimes we seek to move deeper into God's presence by doing something that is connected to our flesh or the natural world. For example, I have experienced instances when God was touching me and I wanted to drink more deeply of His life and thought that by listening to a certain song I would feel more of what the Spirit had been imparting to my soul. But when I went to YouTube to play the song, I wasn't brought into a more fulfilling experience of the blessedness of the Holy One. Instead, I felt disconnected because I sought to access Him by doing something in the flesh rather than just opening up and drinking of His Spirit. Honey on the altar reflects the propensity of human nature to offer up to God, in hopes of a greater encounter with Him, something that represents our flesh.

Another example of how this phenomenon operates in our

lives is thinking that going somewhere or doing something will bring us closer to God. But oftentimes when we go to the place where we think we will encounter Him, we discover that He is no more there than He was at our home.

This law against offering honey on the altar (Lev. 2:11) brings us back to our understanding of the Hebrew word *korban*, which is translated in our English Bibles as "offering" but actually means to draw near. Offering up honey, which again symbolizes the natural energies of the flesh, does not bring us near to God or into the realm of the eternal.

There are many other laws in the early chapters of Leviticus concerning the offerings the priests made. Leviticus 2:13, for instance, states that the offerings had to be salted: "Every grain offering of yours, moreover, you shall season with salt, so that the salt of the covenant of your God shall not be lacking from your grain offering; with all your offerings you shall offer salt."

Salt is a preservative, and the command to salt the offerings points to the fact that God's love and covenant with His people are enduring and will not change, be weakened, or be altered. When we "salt" our offerings, we acknowledge God's everlasting, unchanging covenant made with us through Yeshua, who said, "I will never leave you nor forsake you" (Heb. 13:5, NKJV).

Additionally, Leviticus 6:9 speaks to the fact that fire was to be kept burning continually on the altar: "Command Aaron and his sons, saying, 'This is the law for the burnt offering: the burnt offering itself shall remain on the hearth on the altar all night until the morning, and *the fire on the altar is to be kept burning* on it'" (emphasis added). Keeping a fire going continually involves real work. Wood must be carried and placed upon it at regular intervals. Similarly, to lead a life that is continually being offered up as a sacrifice truly takes much work, effort, and focus.

As we consider the prohibition against offering honey on the altar (Lev. 2:11) and similar commands concerning the offerings of the priests, may we be challenged to recognize the everlasting nature of God's covenant with His people and inspired to keep the fire of our devotion burning brightly as we walk in faithful obedience to Him each day.

THE COMMAND FOR THE PRIESTS TO TAKE CARE OF THEIR APPEARANCE

Then Moses said to Aaron and to his sons Eleazar and Ithamar, "Do not uncover your heads nor tear your clothes."
—LEVITICUS 10:6

IN THIS VERSE, God commanded the priests to maintain a neat and dignified appearance before Him. This signified the attitude of respect they were to show Adonai. Jewish tradition further interprets this mitzvah as prohibiting an excessive growth of long, unkempt hair, emphasizing the need for grooming and personal hygiene. This attention to detail is seen in Ezekiel 44:20, where priests were instructed not to shave their heads entirely nor allow their hair to grow excessively long, but to maintain a controlled and well-groomed appearance.

While this may seem trivial and legalistic, this command reveals God's desire for His people to reflect His glory and holiness in every aspect of our lives, including, as hard as it is for some to accept, the way we present ourselves. It brings to the surface the fact that even the smallest details of our lives matter to the Lord. Again, this is not about legalism but relationship. The point of this instruction is that the priest's appearance was to inspire faith in God, not doubt or discouragement.

In ancient Israel the priests were to be visible representations of God's presence among His people. In a similar way today, neglecting to take care of ourselves or maintain personal hygiene can detract from our witness for Messiah. Have you ever met someone who seems to be radical for Jesus, but they don't cut their lawn, won't wash and take care of their hair, and their house is a chaotic mess? How does that make you feel? Does it encourage your faith in God or leave you discouraged and confused, wondering, "If this person really knows God, why don't they take care of themselves and their property?"

I realize that given our earthly and human limitations, none of us is perfect and there is only so much we can do to control the way we look. But our outer appearance affects our witness of the glory of God. As ambassadors of Christ, our lives should reflect His beauty and excellence in all areas to the best of our ability. By being well-groomed and orderly, we demonstrate the excellency of God.

I remember approximately twenty years ago a woman started attending the congregation I led. It seemed clear that this woman did not consistently brush her teeth because there was so much gunk between her teeth you could not see where one tooth ended and the other began. It was difficult to look at and made one wonder why she didn't have better hygiene. Baruch HaShem, after a few years of her participation in our congregation, she started taking care of herself. She reversed the curse of apathy as it related to her physical appearance, brushing her teeth and dressing attractively. It was a testimony to God's transformative power.

The command for the priests to maintain their appearance (Lev. 10:6) encourages us to honor God in the way we present ourselves. The image of ourselves that we choose to project into the world can be either helpful or harmful for the building of God's kingdom.

THE DEVOTION EXPECTED OF THE PRIESTS

You shall not even go out from the doorway of the tent of meeting...for the LORD's anointing oil is upon you.
—LEVITICUS 10:7

THE TENT OF Meeting was the dwelling place of God among His people, where His presence was tangibly seen and felt. Only those consecrated and anointed for this service could enter the tent—and those who served within *could not depart from it* because of the Lord's anointing upon them.

For example, the high priest was not even allowed to leave the Temple to mourn the deaths of his immediate family members. And the regular priests could not attend a funeral or come in contact with the dead except for their father, mother, brother, unmarried sister, or child. The priests' call and relationship with the Holy One superseded all human relationships. The need to stay undefiled by death was paramount because God is life and the stench of death does not touch Him. Although this law sounds dehumanizing, the high priest's role to be Yahweh's sanctified vessel was more important in the big picture than the emotions of the high priest or his family.

This commandment further illuminates the call for God's priests, which includes you and me (1 Pet. 2:9), to remain in constant communion with Him. The high priest could not come out of the Lord's presence. Similarly, our highest priority should be to stay in continual fellowship with God's Spirit. Every moment is an opportunity to grow and be strengthened in our walk with the Blessed One. We, like the high priest, never leave the temple of God because wherever we are, we strive to stay attached to our Creator.

Everything we walk through in life, both the trials and the pleasures, ought to serve the purpose of bringing us closer to HaShem. As the Scriptures say, "God causes all things to work together for good to those who love God, to those who are called according to His purpose…to [conform us] to the image of His Son" (Rom. 8:28–29). We must never go out of the temple but rather practice the presence of God wherever we go and in whatever we do.

When our focus on God is stable and steadfast, we can say like the Shulamite bride, who is a shadow of the church in the Song of Songs (or Song of Solomon), "Awake, O north wind, and come, wind of the south; make my garden breathe out fragrance, let its spices be wafted abroad. May my beloved come into his garden and eat its choice fruits!" (Song 4:16). In other words, when we make our fellowship with Messiah the priority of our lives, everything we go through—the pleasurable things (the south winds in Song 4:16) and the hard things (the north winds)—will further advance us in our walk with our Maker.

God's Spirit lives inside the soul of everyone who has chosen to follow Yeshua. The Lord is not "out there" somewhere far away. We don't have to go up to the heavens or down to the bottom of the ocean to find Him. He is in our hearts, so near that He is closer than our own breath.

To experience this reality that God's Spirit is literally inside us, we must learn to live from the inside out. We must put down our phones, turn off the TV, stop scrolling through social media, and practice the presence of God. Give Him the first fifteen minutes of the day. Right when you wake up—before you talk with your spouse, kids, or anyone else—sit before the Lord and ask Him to help you get in touch with the reality that His Spirit is living within you. I often listen to soft, soothing worship music as I get still and allow the Holy Spirit to settle my soul and bring me within myself, where He is. In doing this, I remain in the temple. And as I have made this a practice over the years, the Lord has caused me to be led by His Spirit and walk in His power.

The unparalleled devotion required of the high priest in ancient Israel reflected in this command to not leave the Temple (Lev. 10:7) sets a timeless example for us today. Just as the ancient priests were called to consecrate themselves wholly to God's service, so too are we called to let the desire to remain in His presence consume us like fire.

THE PRESCRIPTION FOR CELEBRATING THE DAY OF ATONEMENT

This shall be a permanent statute for you: in the seventh month, on the tenth day of the month, you shall humble your souls and not do any work, whether the native, or the alien who sojourns among you; for it is on this day that atonement shall be made for you to cleanse you; you will be clean from all your sins before the LORD. It is to be a sabbath of solemn rest for you, that you may humble your souls; it is a permanent statute.

—LEVITICUS 16:29–31

THE DAY OF Atonement, described in detail in Leviticus 16, was one of the most significant events in the Israelite religious calendar—a solemn occasion marked by ritualized ceremonies, the forgiveness of sins, and the purification of the people. The intricate instructions given in Leviticus 16 provided a framework for the high priest to carry out the atonement process on behalf of the entire community.

The command to celebrate the Day of Atonement kept the Israelites aware of their need for forgiveness and reconciliation to God. The ritual began with the high priest cleansing himself and his family, followed by the selection of two goats. One goat was designated for sacrifice, while the other became a scapegoat upon which the sins of the people were symbolically transferred.

> Aaron shall cast lots for the two goats, one lot for the LORD and the other lot for the scapegoat.
>
> —LEVITICUS 16:8

The blood of the sacrificial animals served as a temporary atonement for sin, but it was ultimately insufficient to permanently cleanse the conscience of the worshipper (Heb. 10:4). Yeshua, however, offered Himself as the perfect and eternal sacrifice, shedding His blood to atone for the sins of humanity once and for all (Heb. 9:11–14).

Accordingly, the blood of the bull and the goat offered by the high priest on the Day of Atonement prefigured Yeshua's sacrifice on the cross. Just as the blood of the sacrificial animals served as a covering for sin, so does the blood of Yeshua cleanse believers from all unrighteousness (1 John 1:7). His sacrifice accomplished what the blood of bulls and goats could not, providing complete and ultimate forgiveness and reconciliation to God for those who place their faith in Him.

The casting of lots for the two goats, one for the Lord and the other as the scapegoat, illustrates the dual nature of Yeshua's sacrificial work. He is both the sacrifice who takes away the sins of the world and the scapegoat who carries our sins into oblivion (Heb. 9:28).

The Day of Atonement, called in Hebrew Yom Kippur, enlightens us about the gravity of our sin and our need for redemption. Yom Kippur is a day of fasting, repentance, and reflection on one's relationship with God. Similarly, believers in Yeshua are called to examine our hearts, confess our sins, and turn away from that which defiles our relationship with our Maker. "If we *confess our sins*, He is faithful and just to forgive us our sins and to cleanse us from all unrighteousness" (1 John 1:9, emphasis added).

The high priest's meticulous preparation and performance of the ceremonies on the Day of Atonement emphasized the solemnity of the occasion on this sacred day. Its rituals and ceremonies pointed to the ultimate sacrifice of Yeshua, the Messiah, who offered Himself as the perfect atonement for sin. For followers of The Way, the Day of Atonement (Lev. 16) is a call to remember and reflect on the significance of Yeshua's sacrifice while lovingly and gratefully rejoicing in the fact that through Him, we have been made holy and reconciled to God for eternity.

TO LEAVE PART OF ONE'S HARVEST FOR THE POOR AND THE STRANGER

> Now when you reap the harvest of your land, you shall not reap to the very corners of your field, nor shall you gather the gleanings of your harvest....You shall leave them for the needy and for the stranger. I am the LORD your God.
>
> —LEVITICUS 19:9–10

THE PRECEPT TO leave part of one's harvest for the poor and the stranger ensured provision for the less fortunate members of society. This was not supposed to be a onetime act of charity but a continuous lifestyle of giving. By obeying the command to leave the corners of the fields and the gleanings of the harvest, the Israelites reflected God's nature of generosity and compassion, for it was in conjunction with this commandment that Yahweh said, "I am the LORD your God."

We are God's agents of compassion, and He expects us to help meet the needs of the poor. It is interesting that as the four corners of the fields and the fallen fruit from the vineyards were left for the needy, the dignity of those in need was protected. They didn't have to beg or ask for a handout. The food was there for them to take without experiencing humiliation. This highlights the importance of treating the less fortunate with respect and empathy, recognizing their inherent worth as fellow human beings created in the image of God.

As Rabbi Yeshua taught so did the Jewish sages, who said by

the yardstick with which a man measures, by that he is measured. (See also Jesus' teaching in Luke 6:38.) The earth brings forth its crops because God the Creator made it so. The command to leave part of one's harvest for the poor and the stranger (Lev. 19:9–10) illuminates the reality that all things belong to the Lord and we are ministers of His goodness. Just as the earth yields its crops through God's providence, so we are to be channels of His provision and blessing to those around us.

TO NOT DEAL DISHONESTLY WITH OUR FELLOW MAN

You shall not steal, nor deal falsely, nor lie to one another.
—LEVITICUS 19:11

THESE THREE SUCCINCT commandments served as a moral compass for the ancient Israelites. At their core they reflect God's desire for His people to live in harmony and righteousness with one another. By prohibiting stealing, fraudulent dealing, and lying—which includes any form of dishonest acquisition or appropriation—God established a framework for ethical conduct that promotes trust, respect, and justice within the community of Israel. Each of these commands is essential for building strong relationships.

These precepts likewise point us to the importance of integrity in our communication. God desires His beloved to be people of their word, whose speech is honest, sincere, and transparent. Deception, manipulation, and falsehood have no place in the community of faith, as they undermine trust, sow discord, and erode social foundations.

In a broader sense, these commandments challenge us to examine the alignment between our profession of faith and our everyday conduct. There can be a disconnect between religious observance and ethical behavior when we compartmentalize our spirituality and set it apart from our everyday actions. However,

God's commandments leave no room for such hypocrisy. He calls His people to live their faith righteously in every arena.

For believers in Yeshua these commandments to deal honestly with our fellow man (Lev. 19:11) take on even greater significance. Messiah Jesus condemned hypocrisy, deceit, and exploitation, and modeled a life of truthfulness. As His followers we are called to reflect His character, conducting ourselves with integrity, honesty, and fairness in our dealings with others, whether in business, social interactions, or personal relationships.

TO NOT CURSE THE DEAF OR PUT AN OBSTACLE BEFORE THE BLIND

You shall not curse a deaf man, nor place a stumbling block before the blind, but you shall revere your God; I am the LORD.
—LEVITICUS 19:14

THE MITZVAH AGAINST cursing a deaf person or placing a stumbling block before the blind stresses the importance of compassion, empathy, and reverence for God in our interactions with others. This applies particularly to those who are vulnerable, physically weaker, or less powerful in society.

In its original context this law was given to protect the dignity and well-being of individuals with disabilities in a barbaric culture where the weak were vulnerable to being trampled on by the strong and insensitive. Cursing a deaf person or intentionally causing harm to someone who is blind by placing obstacles in their path is, of course, a serious violation of human dignity and a direct affront to the Creator of all humanity. God is very concerned for vulnerable members of society and insists we treat them with compassion and sensitivity.

Many years ago, as a young man, I was working in a men's clothing store. A man came in who had an intellectual disability. Seeing this, the store manager took delight in deceiving him by selling him a synthetic jacket that the manager claimed was made from walrus skin. It was so wrong that even as a young man who didn't know the Lord, I lost all respect for this manager, who was my boss, realizing that he was a very unhealthy, unanchored, and flawed human being.

By showing kindness and compassion to those who are disabled or weak, we demonstrate our reverence and love for God. Messiah Yeshua said, "Truly I tell you, whatever you did for one of the least of these brothers and sisters of mine, you did for me" (Matt. 25:40, NIV). By showing kindness and compassion to those who are disabled or weak, we demonstrate our reverence and love for God.

Romans 12:16 reminds us to "mind not high things, but condescend to men of low estate" (KJV). We must treat all people, regardless of their social status or abilities, with dignity. This acknowledges and celebrates the fact that all people are created in the image of God and worthy of honor.

In Philippians 2:3–4 the apostle Paul exhorts believers to "in humility value others above yourselves, not looking to your own interests but each of you to the interests of the others" (NIV). The commandment against cursing the deaf or placing stumbling blocks before the blind (Lev. 19:14) challenges us to examine our attitudes toward those who are different from us. In a world that values strength, success, and self-interest, we are called to show humility, compassion, and empathy toward everyone, including—and perhaps especially—the disabled and powerless.

By treating the weak and vulnerable with dignity, respect, and kindness, we show that we fear the Holy One and are aware that He is watching. We also reflect the compassionate nature of His character and the atmosphere of the kingdom of God.

TO JUDGE IN RIGHTEOUSNESS

You shall do no injustice in judgment; you shall not be partial to the poor nor defer to the great, but you are to judge your neighbor fairly.
—LEVITICUS 19:15

IN THIS VERSE we encounter a fundamental principle of justice and equity within the legal framework of ancient Israel. This mitzvah proclaims the necessity of impartiality, fairness, and empathy when rendering judgments. It commands us to judge in righteousness, not seeking to gain an advantage by affirming the great, slighting the poor because they cannot help us, or deferring to those with power and influence.

This principle is repeated throughout the Torah, with a similar law found in Deuteronomy 1:17, when Moses charged Israel's judges: "You shall not show partiality in judgment; you shall hear the small and the great alike. You shall not fear man, for the judgment is God's. The case that is too hard for you, you shall bring to me, and I will hear it."

As these commands show, ancient Israel was instructed to administer justice without bias or prejudice. Favoritism toward either the poor or the wealthy was prohibited. Leaders and judges were to treat everyone alike, not fearing any person, regardless of their power or influence. This calls us to a broader commitment to unbiased behavior and decision-making in everyday life. And it challenges us to examine our own tendencies toward prejudice.

At a deeper level, this commandment signals the danger of succumbing to social pressures and personal biases in our interactions. Consider workplace dynamics. Often, individuals may feel inclined to align themselves with influential colleagues or curry favor with superiors, even at the expense of fairness and integrity. Likewise, in social circles the temptation to conform to popular opinions or cater to the preferences of the powerful can lead to unjust treatment of those deemed less significant. We may find ourselves laughing louder at the joke told by an influential person or more readily agreeing with their plans or ideas. In these ways, we subtly make unjust decisions.

The same is true in the other direction. Some people instinctively side with the apparently weak against any form of power or authority. This is just as unhealthy and wrong as thoughtlessly siding with the strong and influential.

The admonition inherent in Leviticus 19:15 drives us to set aside superficial judgments and embrace a higher standard of righteousness. Fairness requires careful consideration of diverse perspectives and circumstances, ensuring that every individual is given a fair hearing and equitable treatment. This echoes the biblical injunction in Proverbs 18:13, "To answer before listening—that is folly and shame" (NIV).

Carrying out this precept to judge in righteousness (Lev. 19:15) can be especially difficult in the face of social pressures to conform. But Messiah taught that fearing man leads to compromise, whereas fearing God leads to wisdom and freedom. In Matthew 10:28, Rabbi Yeshua instructed His disciples, "Do not be afraid of those who kill the body but cannot kill the soul. Rather, be afraid of the One who can destroy both soul and body in hell" (NIV). As we saw previously, when confronted by authorities demanding they stop preaching in Yeshua's name, Peter and the other apostles declared, "We must obey God rather than men" (Acts 5:29).

As believers in Yeshua we are called to embody the character of a just God. Our commitment to fair judgment and impartiality serves as a testimony of His love for each one of us and our commitment to courageously stand for truth in all circumstances.

TO NOT GO ABOUT AS A SLANDERER OR TALEBEARER

You shall not go about as a slanderer among your people, and you are not to act against the life of your neighbor; I am the LORD [Yahweh].
—LEVITICUS 19:16

HONOR AND INTEGRITY in our dealings with others—particularly with regard to our spoken words—matter a great deal to God, as this commandment reveals. It prohibits the spreading of false information or malicious rumors that damage the reputation or well-being of another. Slander, defined as the intentional dissemination of harmful and perhaps misleading information, undermines trust, creates division, and inflicts emotional pain on individuals and communities. By prohibiting slander, this law aims to uphold the dignity of all people, affirming their intrinsic worth as God's creations. The inclusion of "I am the LORD" in this mitzvah emphasizes just how much slander and talebearing run counter to Yahweh's character, which is marked by love, sympathy, empathy, and compassion.

This commandment echoes the teachings of Rabbi Yeshua, who spoke about the power of words, warning us in Matthew 5:22 that whoever calls his brother a "'good-for-nothing,' shall be guilty before the supreme court; and whoever says, 'You fool,' shall be guilty enough to go into the fiery hell."

Back in the 1980s I led a small congregation that held a talent show on the last day of every month. Anyone could get up and sing a song or play an instrument, and it was always such a beautiful time of fellowship. One night I was driving home from one of the talent shows, basking in the presence of the Lord, and then I spoke a negative word about one of the participants. As soon as I did, the peace and sense of God's presence I had been feeling completely left me. That's what speaking negatively will do. Not only will it harm others; it will break our fellowship with God.

This command against going about as a slanderer or talebearer (Lev. 19:16) extends beyond spoken words to include what we say in emails, on social media, and in any other form of communication. In an age of instant connectivity, there are always ready temptations to spread rumors and harm people's character. However, as followers of Yeshua we must exercise restraint in our interactions, taking time to weigh our words and only release ones that carry the love and grace of God. We do well to seek understanding, recognize our own fallibility, and guard the integrity of our communication.

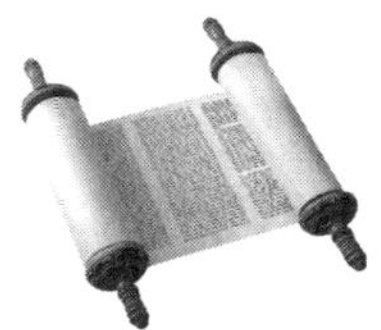

TO NOT HATE OTHER HUMAN BEINGS IN OUR HEARTS

You shall not hate your fellow countryman in your heart.
—LEVITICUS 19:17

THIS PRECEPT ADDRESSES the internal disposition of our hearts, which gives rise to our actions. It admonishes us not to harbor hatred toward our fellowman and urges us to pursue purity of heart in our interpersonal relationships.

As I was writing this in the rabbi's study area off the Western Wall in Jerusalem, a stranger and "fellow countryman" aggressively approached me, jabbing his finger at one of my pens and talking to me in a language I couldn't understand. Without my permission he picked up one of my pens and then pointed to my notebook. He evidently wanted a piece of paper too. In my selfishness I did not want to part with any of my pens or my paper, but I went ahead and gave him what he seemed prepared to take from me. I felt "hatred" for him in my heart—until I looked down at my study materials and started reading about this very mitzvah I am writing about right now! (As I write this, the man just returned my pen!)

This is the value of God's commandments. They sanctify us as we walk through the nitty-gritty details of life. The Scriptures tell us to guard our hearts, for from them flow either life or death (Prov. 4:23). It is interesting that in reference to this command, the rabbis teach that if we feel offended by someone we must go to him, tell him how we feel, give him a chance to explain and possibly apologize, and then forget and forgive.

I personally find that roughly 95 percent of incidents that offend can be resolved through lovingly confronting the one who has hurt us. We explain how we feel and give the person a chance to respond. People in community and relationship cannot function properly unless we are graciously frank and open with one another.

This law to not hate other human beings in our hearts (Lev. 19:17) serves as ballast in the difficult-to-navigate waters of human relationships. It provokes us to resist natural impulses toward hatred and resentment, and to instead establish healthy heart attitudes that yield the fruit of love—even toward those who take our pens!

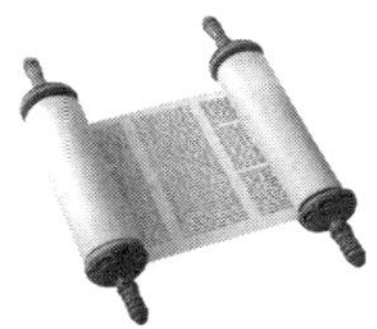

TO REBUKE YOUR NEIGHBOR

You may surely reprove your neighbor, but
shall not incur sin because of him.
—Leviticus 19:17

Not coincidentally, the next commandment tells us to rebuke our neighbors in a spirit of shalom and accountability. Perhaps counterintuitively, this leads to harmony, because we address conflicts directly rather than allowing resentment to fester.

Rabbinic commentary stresses the importance of open communication and reconciliation in resolving conflicts. This wise counsel points us to the transformative power of honest dialogue to bring unity within communities. Honest dialogue has healing potential and paves the way to restoration. While confrontation may seem antithetical to expressions of togetherness, it can be, in fact, evidence of genuine concern for the well-being of others. Grievances, if suppressed and left unaddressed, can sour into bitterness, corroding the bonds of fellowship.

The motivation is always to love. The verse directly after this one, Leviticus 19:18, says, "You shall love your neighbor as yourself." It is amazing how when we rebuke or confront someone who has wronged or hurt us, hearts are mended. But again, if we don't confront and deal with the situation, hatred can grow in our hearts. This is why the Lord says in Leviticus 19:17, don't hate your neighbor (secretly) in your heart, but go challenge him so the bond of love can exist and remain.

As harsh as it may seem, the precept to rebuke our neighbor (Lev. 19:17) calls us to confront others when necessary. This should be done in a spirit of humility, restraint, and discernment. When carried out in a proper way, confrontational dialogue heals and strengthens, leading to greater unity in our relationships.

TO NOT UNNECESSARILY SHAME SOMEONE

You may surely reprove your neighbor, but
shall not incur sin because of him.
—Leviticus 19:17

This precept, although derived from the same verse as the previous law, addresses another matter. While it is important to deal with wrongdoing, it is equally important not to needlessly shame or degrade the person being challenged. The balance between honest confrontation and upholding the dignity of those involved is critical in the spiritual and communal laws prescribed in the Torah.

The rabbis teach that you rebuke only as publicly and strongly as the situation demands, endeavoring to not unnecessarily shame the one you rebuke. We must also be mindful, however, that sometimes severe confrontation and that which seems harsh are necessary. This was demonstrated in Paul's instruction to Timothy: "Those who continue in sin, rebuke in the presence of all, so that the rest also will be fearful of sinning" (1 Tim. 5:20). But to rebuke someone from a wrong motivation or a lack of self-control, or even just to make fun of them, is considered a terrible evil.

Addressing conflicts is sometimes necessary; however, needlessly shaming, or correcting, someone can have long-lasting effects on the person's mind, emotions, and standing within the community. It usually leads to division, alienation, and resentment. The wisdom of this commandment is its call for a proportional response—one that fits the severity of the situation without crossing into cruelty or humiliation. Rebukes must be measured and mindful, not reckless and damaging. Confrontation is an opportunity for constructive interaction motivated by genuine concern for all parties.

Implemented rightly, this mitzvah to avoid unnecessarily shaming someone (Lev. 19:17) helps develop compassionate and empathetic communities where members feel safe and valued, even when they falter. It encourages a culture where mistakes are viewed as opportunities for growth and learning rather than occasions for punishment or exclusion. The enduring result is a stronger social fabric made so by the courage to confront in humility and with a heart for restoration.

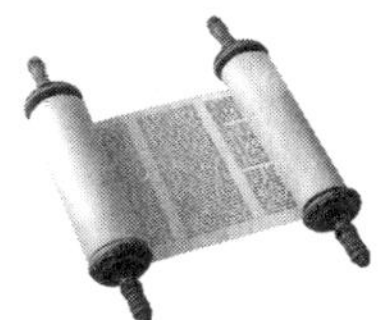

TO NOT TAKE REVENGE

You shall not take vengeance.
—Leviticus 19:18

This commandment pinpoints one of the most instinctive and destructive reactions to being wronged: the desire for revenge. Scripture distinguishes between constructive rebuke and acts of vengeance, with one seeking to heal and uphold, and the other to harm and tear down.

"Vengeance is Mine," says the Lord in Deuteronomy 32:35 and Romans 12:19. The sin of carrying out our own vengeance involves hypocrisy because we also are guilty of sin, as Messiah pointed out to the ones who tried to stone the adulteress in John 8:7. We are constantly committing wrongs against God, yet He is longsuffering and compassionate toward you and me. Additionally, we cannot see deep enough beneath the surface to judge with true understanding. We may want to take revenge on an abuser without recognizing that people often become abusers because they themselves were abused.

This command to not take vengeance (Lev. 19:18) comes immediately after God's command to challenge or "reprove" somebody who does wrong (Lev. 19:17). This points out the difference between a spirit of revenge and destruction, and a spirit that confronts to heal and restore. Read all of Leviticus 19:17–18: "You shall not hate your fellow countryman in your heart; you may surely reprove your neighbor, but shall not incur sin because of him. You shall not take vengeance, nor bear any grudge against the sons of your people, but you shall love your neighbor as yourself; I am the LORD."

Notice these two verses end with, "You shall love your neighbor as yourself; I am the LORD." What timeless words! Revenge can seem like a satisfying response to grievances, but it ultimately perpetuates conflict and departs from the ethical principles set forth in the Torah. Instead, God calls us to a higher standard where forgiveness and restraint are the pathways to resolving conflicts.

The prohibition against taking revenge (Lev. 19:18) is a fundamental precept that promotes spiritual and relational health. It challenges us to rise above our baser instincts and look to the perfect Judge who, in time, will set right every injustice done to us and others in His merciful and understanding way.

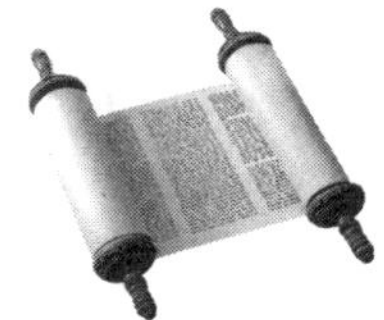

TO NOT BEAR A GRUDGE

You shall not take vengeance, nor *bear any grudge* against the sons of your people.
—Leviticus 19:18, emphasis added

Even as vengeance is forbidden, as we saw in the previous law, so are grudges. We are not allowed to harbor unforgiving attitudes and motivations toward others.

The rabbis give the following classic examples of what it means to hold a grudge. Person A comes to his friend, B, to borrow a hatchet, but B refuses to lend it to him. The next day, B comes to A to borrow a knife, but A says, "You refused to lend me the hatchet yesterday, so why should I lend you the knife today?" Even if person A replied, "I will lend you my knife today even though you wouldn't lend me your hatchet yesterday," it still would indicate that he was thinking about the wrong done to him and thus holding a grudge.

Sometimes our actions can be right even when our hearts are wrong. Paul addressed this as it relates to honoring the Lord with our finances: "Each one must do just as he has purposed in his heart, not *grudgingly* or under compulsion, for God loves a cheerful giver" (2 Cor. 9:7, emphasis added). We can do the right thing but with bitterness or resentment, so the Lord here is asking us to not just do the right thing but to do it with a pure heart.

This commandment takes on even greater spiritual depth in

light of Rabbi Yeshua's teachings. He made forgiveness a cornerstone of His gospel, famously expanding on the Torah's precepts by instructing His followers to love their enemies and pray for those who persecute them (Matt. 5:44). This radical call to transcend the natural urge to hold a grudge and instead release those who have offended us transforms personal relationships and prioritizes the need for believers to show mercy.

The benefits are corporate and personal. True forgiveness, in which we leave the ultimate consequences to God, produces heartfelt peace. It liberates individuals and groups from the bondage of bitterness and anger. Our great example is Yeshua, whose love for us led Him to sacrifice His life on the cross for our sins, which was the ultimate act of forgiveness.

In practical terms, the application of this precept involves daily decisions to overlook offenses, let go of past hurts, and choose forgiveness, even when it feels undeserved. This is a deliberate choice to reflect the character of Yeshua.

For the Jewish community and all God's people today, this command plays a vital role in forming ethical, harmonious societies. This mitzvah reinforces the universal call to extend grace in all relationships. It challenges our self-absorbed and egotistical tendencies toward revenge and retaliation, promoting the godly and ascended ethos of reconciliation and shalom.

The commandment not to bear a grudge (Lev. 19:18), illuminated by the teachings of Rabbi Yeshua, calls us all to a higher standard of interpersonal conduct that mirrors the forgiving nature of God Himself.

TO LOVE YOUR NEIGHBOR AS YOURSELF

You shall love your neighbor as yourself; I am the LORD.
—LEVITICUS 19:18

THIS TIMELESS COMMAND encapsulates the teaching of the Torah and is foundational to all the Law and the Prophets. In fact, an ancient Jewish sage taught that this command is a pillar upon which the Torah has been built.

For Jews, this command expresses the essence of the Torah's social laws and defines community relations and personal behavior. It calls us to act in ways that support the well-being of others. In fact, when we study Hasidic Jewish communities, we find that the needs of everyone within those communities are taken care of by the community at large.

Rabbi Yeshua also identified this mitzvah as one of the two greatest commandments. When asked, "Which is the greatest commandment in the Law?" He responded by saying: "'You shall love the Lord your God with all your heart, and with all your soul, and with all your mind.' This is the great and foremost commandment. The second is like it, 'You shall love your neighbor as yourself.' On these two commandments depend the whole Law and the Prophets" (Matt. 22:36–40).

If you think about it, every law we have gone through directs us either to love God through our obedience and devotion or to love our neighbor (our fellow man). When we read Leviticus 19:18, "You shall love your neighbor as yourself," the question naturally occurs, *Who is our neighbor?* In Luke 10:27–37 a lawyer asked Messiah Jesus this very question. In reply Yeshua told the story of how a man was robbed, beaten, and left for dead along the side of the road. A priest and then a Levite passed by him and didn't help. But an average person, the Good Samaritan, stopped and helped him. Yeshua's point—everybody is our neighbor.

Although simple, this commandment belies its transformative power in society. To love one's neighbor as oneself means extending to others the same type of care, consideration, respect, and love we naturally have for ourselves.

Yeshua's teachings and example extend this mitzvah well into the realm of sacrifice. His death on the cross was the ultimate act of love toward one's neighbors. "Greater love has no one than this, that one lay down his life for his friends" (John 15:13).

This law to love your neighbor as yourself (Lev. 19:18) challenges us to consider how our actions, decisions, and words affect others. Are we speaking and behaving in the ways we want done to us? This simple, profound test of love can continually transform our lives.

THE PROHIBITION AGAINST FORBIDDEN MIXTURES

You shall keep my statutes. You shall not let your cattle breed with a different kind. You shall not sow your field with two kinds of seed, nor shall you wear a garment of cloth made of two kinds of material.
—Leviticus 19:19, esv

This command speaks to the idea that we should limit the creativity God has given us to the boundaries He established in creation rather than altering His original design and blueprint. Tampering with God's creation is forbidden in Jewish law. Crossbreeding animals, for example, produces new species God did not originally create, potentially disrupting the natural balance He set. A "wolfdog," for instance, a cross between a dog and a wolf, is forbidden. Plants like the "tangelo"—the result of crossing a grapefruit and a tangerine—and the "Tom-Tato," which can produce both tomatoes and potatoes from the same stem, also fall into this category. And the list goes on.

The great Torah scholar Maimonides taught that garments made from mixing different kinds of materials were worn by idolatrous priests, and we are forbidden from following in their ways. Other rabbinic sources say that "mixing wool and linen is akin to mixing, and unleashing, the spiritual forces associated respectively with Cain and Abel, and can have damaging results."[9]

God created the world with wisdom to serve His divine purpose. Scripture says, "God saw all that He had made, and behold, it was very good" (Gen. 1:31). Only the Lord has the right to produce or create new species of life. Experimentation and meddling with His creative process puts man in the dangerous position of playing God.

In contemporary times one has to wonder how the principle in this precept relates to AI (artificial intelligence). AI is created programs and code that can cause computers to function with seeming intelligence. Industry experts and many others believe its impact on health care, automation, communication, and space exploration can improve our lives and make us more productive. But although initially AI may appear to offer convenience and advancement, it carries the risk of creating a world that loses touch with both a holy God and authentic human experience.

AI systems may become "smarter" than humans, thinking for themselves and taking on lives of their own. Some leading experts in this field fear the technology could turn on us and end up destroying the world. A professor at Oxford warns that "there is a grave risk of artificial intelligence breaking free of human control and turning on its creators."[10] The quest to transcend the Creator's natural boundaries through technology and innovation can lead to unforeseen consequences, distancing us from God's order and purpose.

The Lord put limits on what mankind should tamper with. We started by crossbreeding plants and animals, then we began to try to clone human beings, and now we have created AI to think independently of God and man. It is foolish and dangerous to transgress God's laws. The Most High has His reasons for setting boundaries and warning man not to alter His divine design that He built into creation.

When Yahweh's laws were originally handed down, it was difficult to understand why some of them, including this law, were given. Rashi, the renowned Jewish commentator from the eleventh century, noted that obeying the mitzvot, even without knowing the reasoning, is the highest form of devotion.

Obedience in the absence of full understanding demonstrates a deep trust in the wisdom and sovereignty of Adon Olam.

This raises an introspective question. Do you and I obey God when He is leading us to do something we don't understand, or do we yield to Him only when we fully comprehend His ways? Abraham obeyed Adonai not knowing where He was leading him, and by so doing Abraham received his inheritance (Heb. 11:18). It is noteworthy to consider that Abraham is called the father of all who believe (Rom. 4). This hints at the fact that if we are true believers, we must walk like Abraham, obeying the Blessed One even when we can't understand His directives.

This commandment also serves as a metaphor for not mixing the truths of the gospel with secular beliefs or becoming "unequally yoked" with unbelievers in ways that might compromise our faith (2 Cor. 6:14). For both Jews and Gentiles, the law prohibiting forbidden mixtures sounds a call for us to fully align with God's principles and avoid the spiritual contamination that can occur when divine standards are mingled with worldly values.

By adhering to the revelation in God's instruction prohibiting forbidden mixtures (Lev. 19:19), we demonstrate our absolute trust in HaShem, the Master of the World, and our respect for the natural order and boundaries He has set.

THE PROHIBITION AGAINST DIVINATION, SOOTHSAYING, AND OTHER OCCULT PRACTICES

You shall not...practice divination or soothsaying.
—Leviticus 19:26

This commandment demands that spiritual guidance and wisdom be sought from God alone. In ancient Israel, divination and soothsaying were commonly used among the neighboring cultures in an attempt to gain insight into future events. By prohibiting these activities, the Torah set Israel apart in its devotion to Yahweh, the one true God.

The spiritual practices God's covenant people were to avoid include the following:

- Divination—seeking knowledge by supernatural means, which today would include practices like reading tarot cards and fortune-telling
- Soothsaying—making one's plans dependent on the position of the stars, through astrology, for instance
- Witchcraft—manipulating people or circumstances through supernatural means or methods other than God

- The use of mediums or talking (and praying) to the dead—we see an example of this in 1 Samuel 28:7–12, where Saul called on a medium to bring Samuel from the dead to advise him

Signaling the importance of this law is the fact that a similar mitzvah is found in Deuteronomy 18:10–13: "There shall not be found among you anyone who makes his son or his daughter pass through the fire, one who uses divination, one who practices witchcraft, or one who interprets omens, or a sorcerer, or one who casts a spell, or a medium, or a spiritist, or one who calls up the dead. For whoever does these things is detestable to the LORD; and because of these detestable things the LORD your God will drive them out before you. You shall be blameless before the LORD your God."

Many people who profess to follow Yeshua talk to and even pray to their dead relatives, referring to them as their "angels" who watch over them. Some engage in what they think are harmless spiritual practices such as horoscope reading, astrology, palm-reading, "aura" reading, and other pursuits that fall outside the bounds of scriptural instruction.

All of this is forbidden. According to the rabbis, even the practice of creating optical illusions to make it seem like one is performing "magic" is wrong and evil. Magic takes people's focus off God alone, who is the true miracle worker.

For Jews and Gentiles alike, this prohibition against divination, soothsaying, and other occult practices (Lev. 19:26) underscores a broader spiritual truth: We must rely on God alone, and this requires faith. Divination and soothsaying represent a lack of faith and a desire to control or predict circumstances apart from Adonai. This commandment calls us to depend on Yahweh, to seek Him and wait on Him for guidance without resorting to other means to gain knowledge or power. We must trust, as

Isaiah 46:10 says, that His purpose will be established in our lives and He will accomplish all His good pleasure.

HaShem has good plans for His children, plans to prosper us and not to harm us (Jer. 29:11). We don't need to turn to unholy means when we are in covenant relationship with the one true God.

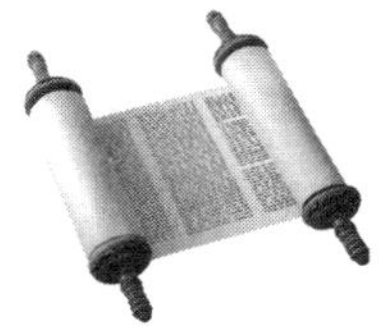

THE PROHIBITION AGAINST SHAVING THE CORNERS OF THE HEAD AND BEARD

You shall not round off the side-growth of your heads nor harm the edges of your beard.
—Leviticus 19:27

In its ancient cultural context this commandment distinguished the appearance of male Israelites from their neighbors. Israelite men were commanded to let the hair in the front of their ears grow so it extends past the cheekbones, resulting in sidelocks, which in Hebrew are called *peyos*. Some Jewish men grow them long as a way of emphasizing this commandment, to appear pious, or simply as a way of self-identifying as a Jew. As one source noted, sidelocks, or *peyos*, are signs that proclaim, "I am a Jew. I am not *of* this world, even if I am *in* this world. I am a Jew."[11]

Personally, my *peyos* are a continual reminder to me of my unique relationship with God.

The reason for this commandment is not clearly stated in the Torah. It has been suggested that many cultures in that day engaged in specific grooming practices associated with idolatry, which may have included the cutting of their sideburns. By forbidding such practices, the Torah asserted Israel's unique relationship with God and their status as His set-apart, chosen people.

This commandment also affirms God's creative order by keeping men distinct from women. Men are not permitted to shave their beards, according to this mitzvah, because beards distinguish men from women. Unfortunately, today the beautiful and God-ordained distinction between men and women is being blurred. In our present culture, for example, some men wear their jeans so tight that at first glance you think you are looking at a woman. And on the other side of the coin, some women both dress and cut their hair like men. Paul addressed this in 1 Corinthians 11:6, writing, "It is disgraceful for a woman to have her hair cut off."

The crisis of gender-identity confusion is exploding all around us, and gender dysphoria is common. As we know, social media sites now offer gender choices such as "male, female, or other." In many cases "other" has been changed to "custom," with a blank field to enter your own gender label. Slogans such as "Anatomy isn't destiny" are defining this generation. We are living in days of tremendous confusion.

Despite what this world tells us, there are God-ordained differences between men and women, and these distinctions must be preserved. For example, Deuteronomy 22:5 says, "A woman shall not wear man's clothing, nor shall a man put on a woman's clothing; for whoever does these things is an abomination to the LORD your God." This law isn't saying women can't wear pants but rather is forbidding cross-dressing and behaving like a member of the opposite sex. Our Creator is not sexist; He is loving and compassionate. When we choose to throw off godly restraint and step out of alignment with the Blessed One's eternal wisdom and order that He built into creation, chaos and suffering will follow.

Both men and women are created in God's image and equally reflect His glory: "God created man in His own image, in the image of God He created him; male and female He created them" (Gen. 1:27). We must appreciate and honor the biological sex we were given at birth and cultivate it.

The prohibition against shaving the corners of the head and

beard (Lev. 19:27), therefore, serves as a call to all believers to maintain a biblical worldview and not be sucked into today's unisex culture. We are to value our differences as men and women, and maintain the distinctiveness between the sexes and between maleness and femaleness.

TO RESPECT GOD'S SANCTUARY

You shall...revere My sanctuary; I am the LORD.
—LEVITICUS 19:30

IN THE CONTEXT of ancient Israel, this command highlighted the sanctity of the Tabernacle (and later the Temple in Jerusalem) and instructed the Israelites to approach it with a sense of worship and profound regard. The priests of Israel would perform their duties in the Temple barefoot, demonstrating an attitude of holy awe and reverence. Similarly, some Jews today walk backward when leaving the Western Wall in Jerusalem so they don't turn their back toward the place where God's holy Temple once stood. A great example of honor and respect!

It should be pointed out that today's synagogues are loosely patterned after the Tabernacle, which this verse refers to as "God's sanctuary." One similarity is that in modern Orthodox synagogues, prayer services are held at the same times the daily sacrifices were offered in the Tabernacle and later the Temple. Additionally, the ark in the synagogue (called *aron kodesh* in Hebrew, meaning "the holy ark"), which houses the Torah scroll, symbolically represents the Holy of Holies in God's original sanctuary, the Tabernacle.

Although the ancient Tabernacle and Temple are no longer standing, this mitzvah provides a standard for us today. By fostering an attitude of respect for places of worship, we are better able to receive God's Word because our hearts are in a right posture. I often lament, "How have we gone from having reverence for houses of worship to drinking coffee in the pews?" Our approach is often far too casual and inappropriate when we assemble to worship and meet with the Lord our God.

When Moses encountered the Lord, God said to him, "Remove your sandals from your feet, for the place on which you are standing is holy ground" (Exod. 3:5). I understand and love the grace message, but have we lost the sense of reverence that is appropriate for worshipping our holy Father? I often think so. If you were invited to the White House, would you walk into the president's office with a paper cup filled with coffee in your hand? Surely not.

In the New Testament, Rabbi Yeshua highlighted this lack of reverence when He cleansed the Temple, driving out those who had turned it into a marketplace. Messiah cried out, quoting Isaiah, "My house shall be called a house of prayer" (Matt. 21:13).

This command to respect God's sanctuary (Lev. 19:30) should wake us up to the fact that although God is our friend, He is not just a buddy. He is the Lord and should be approached as the Holy One when we assemble together in our houses of worship.

TO RESPECT THE AGED AND WISE

You shall rise up before the grayheaded and honor
the aged, and you shall revere your God.
—Leviticus 19:32

This command is not simply advocating a form of social etiquette but speaks to our attitude toward the elderly. In a culture where the young are celebrated and the aged are too often cast aside, where youth is worshipped and growing old is viewed as a handicap, we must resist this godless mindset by consciously honoring our senior citizens.

To "rise up" before the elderly, as this law states, is more than just a gesture of deference; it acknowledges the intrinsic value and dignity of those who are older than us and have lived through many decades and cultural changes. It honors their life experiences, insights, and contributions, recognizing them as repositories of wisdom and knowledge. While our society dismisses the elderly, this mitzvah reminds us to celebrate and respect their inherent worth and the significance of what they have gained and become over the course of an extended life.

The rabbinic tradition emphasizes the importance of honoring not only the elderly but also those who possess wisdom and counsel, regardless of their age. It is stated in the rabbinic literature, "Even an old man must rise when a sage passes by," especially if the sage is his principal instructor.[12] A sage is an individual who possesses profound wisdom. Biblical culture is one of respect and honor for all individuals and especially those who are God's channels to bring holy light into the earth. This is the reason Paul wrote, "The elders who rule well are to be considered worthy of double honor, especially those who work hard at preaching and teaching" (1 Tim. 5:17).

This precept to respect the aged and wise (Lev. 19:32) challenges us to cultivate a culture of honor for the elderly by valuing their wisdom, experience, and perspectives. We discern in this mitzvah the profound spiritual truth that in honoring the aged and wise, we honor God Himself. He is the Source of all wisdom and knowledge (Prov. 2:6), and the elderly and wise are vessels through whom His wisdom is imparted.

TO ENGAGE IN FAIR BUSINESS DEALINGS

> You shall have just balances, just weights, a just ephah, and a just hin; I am the LORD your God.
> —LEVITICUS 19:36

THIS DIRECTIVE CALLED the Israelites to have integrity and be honest in their business practices. They were to apply "just weights" and not exploit others, thus reflecting God's character and His desire that His people embody righteousness in all their dealings.

We have a similar commandment in Deuteronomy 25: "You shall not have in your bag differing weights, a large and a small.... You shall have a full and just weight; you shall have a full and just measure, that your days may be prolonged in the land which the LORD your God gives you" (vv. 13, 15). Figuratively speaking, this is equivalent to pressuring someone to sell us goods below market value, and then turning around and reselling the item at an unfair price to a naïve soul. Being just in our business dealings and how we handle money is a direct reflection of the true quality of our character and is very important to our Maker. In Proverbs 16:11 we read about how important our business transactions are to God: "A just balance and scales belong to the LORD; all the weights of the bag are His concern."

A lack of integrity in business practices pervades modern culture and spans from cheating on our income taxes, to HVAC companies wanting to replace our whole air-conditioning units when simply replacing a part would suffice, to automobile mechanics recommending services that are not truly necessary. Of course, not all HVAC companies or auto mechanics are dishonest. My point is only that the disregard for the Holy One's command to practice integrity in our business dealings is widespread and has affected many of us.

I had a friend who was advised to refinance his house by a mortgage broker who wanted to make a commission, and it ended up costing my naïve friend thousands of dollars. Unfortunately, many of God's people not only have been taken advantage of but also have been guilty of not using "just weights and measures" and have taken advantage of others. I knew a man many years ago who paid someone to roll the speedometer back in his car so he could make more money when he sold it. This is the exact type of behavior this law is addressing. It is all too tempting to engage in deceptive practices for financial gain.

Unfortunately, being a self-proclaimed believer doesn't always mean someone has good or fair business practices. Like me, you may have seen directories of "Christian businesses." Unfortunately, after engaging the services of several of these "Christian" businesses, I discovered that just because a business advertises itself as Christian, that doesn't necessarily mean it is honest and competent. There can be no "spiritual schizophrenics" who profess a relationship with HaShem but are dishonest in their dealings with humanity.

God is never unfair. He never cheats people or cuts corners, and He forbids us from dealing dishonestly in financial matters. By obeying this precept to engage in fair business dealings (Lev. 19:36), we express our respect for our Father and faith in Him to meet our needs.

TO AVOID HEATHEN CUSTOMS

Moreover, you shall not follow the customs of the nation which I will drive out before you.
—Leviticus 20:23

In ancient times the Israelites were surrounded by nations that were steeped in idolatry and immorality. This commandment served as a safeguard against assimilation and syncretism, preserving the purity of Israel's worship and preventing spiritual defilement from pagan customs.

This mitzvah is one reason Daniel didn't worship Babylon's god, eat what they ate, or dress like they dressed—he was uniquely different. Even today Hasidic Jews dress the way they do to be different and not conform to the nations around them. We too must be in the world but not of it.

Like Israel, we are not to emulate the world around us. We are holy. Many of the customs and values in the culture that surrounds us are being projected into the world by powers of darkness. The spiritual energies behind lawlessness, lewdness, immoral sensuality, addiction, and rebellion, to name a few, are drawing humanity into the outer darkness, a place of unfathomable torment (Matt. 8:12).

This is why the Lord warns in Jeremiah 51:6, "Flee from the midst of Babylon, and each of you save his life! Do not be destroyed in her punishment, for this is the Lord's time of vengeance; He is going to render recompense to her." And in Leviticus 20:23 He says, "You shall not follow the customs of the nation which I will drive out before you, for they did all these things [broke God's Law], and therefore I have abhorred them." So too are we to forsake the world from which the Father has saved us. He says, "Come out from the world. Draw near to Me, and I will receive you to Myself." (See 2 Corinthians 6:17 and James 4:8.)

The commandment to avoid heathen customs must be understood in light of spiritual warfare. Our struggle is not against flesh and blood but against spiritual forces of darkness (Eph. 6:12). We must resist subtle demonic influences that are seeking to steal and corrupt our souls. This means engaging the culture we are surrounded by with discernment, evaluating every practice, attitude, and tradition in light of Scripture.

This mitzvah to avoid heathen customs (Lev. 20:23) calls us to embrace our identity as children of the Most High and to walk in obedience to His precepts. There's a price to pay if we do not:

> After these things I saw another angel coming down from heaven, having great authority, and the earth was illumined with his glory. And he cried out with a mighty voice, saying, "Fallen, fallen is Babylon the great! She has become a dwelling place of demons and a prison of every unclean spirit, and a prison of every unclean and hateful bird. For all the nations have drunk of the wine of the passion of her immorality, and the kings of the earth have committed acts of immorality with her, and the merchants of the earth have become rich by the wealth of her sensuality."
>
> I heard another voice from heaven, saying, "Come out of her, my people, so that you will not participate in her sins and receive of her plagues."
>
> —Revelation 18:1–4

God, help us all!

TO RESPECT THE SANCTITY OF OFFERINGS

They shall not profane the holy gifts of the sons of Israel which they offer to the Lord, and so cause them to bear punishment for guilt by eating their holy gifts; for I am the Lord who sanctifies them.
—Leviticus 22:15–16

In ancient Israel the sanctity of offerings was paramount. Sacrifices were central to Israel's worship and served as a means of atonement for sin, reconciliation with God, and dedication to God's service. Any misuse or mishandling of these offerings not only dishonored the Lord but also incurred His righteous judgment upon the people. Thus, the priests were to treat the gifts God's people offered to the Lord with devotion and respect.

This command also made the priest responsible for ensuring that the animals being brought to the Lord as offerings were not being eaten in a common way, as if the holy offerings were simply a meal.

A parallel could be made here in the way we partake of the sacraments of Communion. If we are not careful, we can partake of the bread (matzo) and juice in such a way as to profane it and bring judgment upon ourselves. Paul wrote in 1 Corinthians 11, "Therefore whoever eats the bread or drinks the cup of the Lord in an unworthy manner, shall be guilty of the body and the blood of the Lord. But a man must examine himself, and in so doing he is to eat of the bread and drink of the cup. For he who eats and drinks, eats and drinks judgment to himself if he does not judge the body rightly" (vv. 27–29).

Thus, the command to respect the sanctity of offerings (Lev. 22:15–16) challenges us to examine our hearts to ensure that our offerings and worship are authentic expressions of honor to the Blessed One.

ALL ANIMALS OFFERED TO THE LORD HAD TO BE WITHOUT DEFECT

Any man of the house of Israel or of the aliens in Israel who presents his offering...for you to be accepted—it must be a male without defect....Whatever has a defect, you shall not offer, for it will not be accepted for you....It must be perfect to be accepted.
—Leviticus 22:18–21

This command reflects the broader biblical principle that God deserves our best in everything. The requirement for animals to be without defect symbolizes the perfection required in offerings given to God, pointing to the holiness and purity that should characterize anything devoted to Him.

The writings of the Hebrew prophet Malachi further expand this point:

> "'A son honors his father, and a servant his master. Then if I am a father, where is My honor? And if I am a master, where is My respect?' says the Lord of hosts to you, O priests who despise My name. But you say, 'How have we despised Your name?' You are presenting defiled food upon My altar....But *when you present the blind for sacrifice, is it not evil? And when you present the lame and sick, is it not evil?* Why not offer it to your governor? Would he be pleased with you? Or

> would he receive you kindly?" says the LORD of hosts.
>
> —MALACHI 1:6–8, EMPHASIS ADDED

In Judaism, the law requiring animals offered to the Lord to be without defect is connected to the Hebrew word *tāmîm*, which is translated "perfect" or "without blemish."[13] This means the animal had to be free from any physical imperfections or injuries that would render it unsuitable for sacrifice. One source notes that "the requirement that priests and sacrifices should be without blemish was common to all the ancient civilizations, and there is evidence of this from Egypt, Mesopotamia, Hatti (the land of the Hittites), Greece, and Rome. Egyptian documents state that candidates for the priesthood were examined for blemishes, and that the sacrifices were examined in the same way, marking animals fit for sacrifice."[14]

Our goal is perfection because God is perfect. This is why Yeshua said, "Therefore you are to be perfect, as your heavenly Father is perfect" (Matt. 5:48). We are on a journey toward perfection, and in our spirits we should settle for nothing less. As Paul wrote, "Not that I have already obtained it or have already become perfect, but I press on so that I may lay hold of that for which also I was laid hold of by Christ Jesus" (Phil. 3:12). The goal of perfection is unity and deep fellowship with our Maker.

In the Brit Chadashah (New Testament), Yeshua is revealed as the perfect, unblemished, eternal offering for sin (Heb. 7–10). Unlike the repeated and imperfect sacrifices made under the old covenant, Messiah's sacrifice once and for all atoned for sin.

Through Him we have imputed perfection now (2 Cor. 5:21), and our full perfection will manifest in the age to come, called in Hebrew *Olam HaBa*, meaning "the World to Come."[15]

> Beloved, now we are children of God, and it has not appeared as yet what we will be. We know that when He appears, we

> will be like Him, because we will see Him just as He is.
>
> —1 JOHN 3:2

As this law commanded animals offered to Yahweh to be without defect (Lev. 22:18–21), so Yeshua offered Himself up for us as our perfect sacrifice, securing our redemption. Furthermore, we as living sacrifices are being perfected so there will be no defect in us. We will be presented before Him perfect and complete, for as Paul wrote: "I am confident of this very thing, that He who began a good work in you will perfect it until the day of Christ Jesus" (Phil. 1:6).

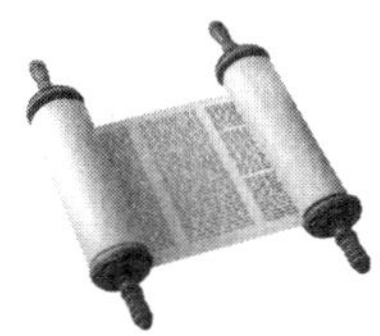

TO LIVE IN A WAY THAT DOES NOT PROFANE GOD'S NAME

So you shall keep My commandments, and do them; I am the Lord. You shall not profane My holy name, but I will be sanctified among the sons of Israel; I am the Lord who sanctifies you, who brought you out from the land of Egypt, to be your God; I am the Lord.
—Leviticus 22:31–33

After giving His children a long list of commandments in Leviticus, God instructs them to not profane His name. They were to be diligent to sanctify it. It is critical to honor God's name in word and deed, because His name represents His character and authority.

God's name can be profaned by

- speaking it in a way that is casual and without proper reverence;
- bringing shame to it by identifying oneself as a believer but living ungodly;
- using it as a curse word;
- taking an oath in His name; or
- doing evil in God's name or engaging in anything that causes Him to be disrespected.

In Judaism, the opposite of profaning God's name is sanctifying it, a concept that in Hebrew is called *Kiddush HaShem*. We do this by living in a way that reflects His light—having godly character, doing good, speaking truth, lifting Him up, and drawing others to Him. Any action that brings honor, respect, and glory to God is *Kiddush HaShem*—sanctifying His name. In contrast, any behavior or action that disgraces or harms God's reputation is called in Hebrew *Chillul HaShem*—desecration of His name.

As followers of Yeshua, we profane God's name when we who are created in His image don't walk in His ways. How can we curse, swear, and yell at people habitually, whether we are targeting those closest to us or those we encounter in the course of our days? How can we continually murmur, complain, and criticize, and yet call ourselves Spirit-filled believers? How can we as Christians wear T-shirts with the names of musical groups whose songs include ungodly lyrics?

In the original context the profaning of God's name followed the command to offer a proper sacrifice, because when an improper sacrifice is offered, His name is profaned. But we must remember that today you and I are His sacrifices, and we must present ourselves to God authentically. Believers are called to live worthy of the calling we have received—in a manner that brings glory rather than ridicule to God.

Sanctifying the Blessed One's name is not merely about avoiding actions that bring dishonor to God but about actively engaging in life in ways that highlight His supreme holiness, beauty, and glory. It is a dynamic, ongoing way of living so people around us can't help but notice God's presence in us.

In ancient Israel this command extended beyond individual morality to corporate identity and witness. Every aspect of communal life, from judicial decisions to the way they treated the poor and the stranger, was to sanctify HaShem by reflecting His character.

In addition, the sanctification of God's name involves our verbal testimony. When we recount what God has done in our lives and in the world, we exalt His name in praise and invite others to recognize His power and mercy.

This command to sanctify rather than profane God's name (Lev. 22:31–33) challenges us to take seriously how we project ourselves in the world. Our lifestyles, decisions, and interactions with others all honor or dishonor the Lord. This means we must put a careful watch on our words and choices, big and small. Like ancient Israel, we are called to make God's name glorious in the earth.

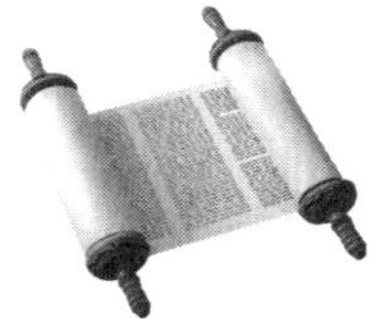

THE PRECEPT TO CELEBRATE AND HONOR GOD'S FEASTS

Speak to the children of Israel, and say to them: "The feasts of the LORD, which you shall proclaim to be holy convocations, these are My feasts."
—LEVITICUS 23:2, NKJV

IN LEVITICUS 23 the Lord commands His people, Israel, to keep His holy days: the Sabbath (Shabbat, v. 3), Passover (v. 5), the Feast of Unleavened Bread (v. 6), the Feast of Firstfruits (vv. 10–11), Pentecost (Shavuot, vv. 15–16), the Feast of Trumpets (v. 24), the Day of Atonement (Yom Kippur, v. 27), and the Feast of Tabernacles (Sukkot, vv. 34–42). Historically, these holy, or appointed, days commemorated significant events in Israel's history and served as a time to gather and remember God's deliverance and blessings. Yet each of these holy days finds its ultimate fulfillment in Yeshua.

In Leviticus 23 the Lord commanded His people to remember the **Sabbath**: "For six days work may be done, but on the seventh day there is a sabbath of complete rest, a holy convocation....You shall do no laborious work. It is to be a perpetual statute in all your dwelling places throughout your generations" (vv. 3, 21). The Hebrew word for the Sabbath is *Shabbat*, which is a day of rest. In Judaism, Shabbat begins on Friday just before sunset and ends on the following evening after nightfall. The reason it begins in the evening instead of the morning is that this is the pattern recorded in the Creation account. In Genesis chapter 1, six times we read the phrase, "And there was evening and there was morning," referring to the span of one day (vv. 5, 8, 13, 19, 23, 31).

While God established the Sabbath at creation when He rested on the seventh day (Gen. 2:2–3), for ancient Israel the Sabbath rest was also a commemoration of their liberation from slavery in Egypt, where rest was not afforded to them. Deuteronomy 5:15 declares: "You shall remember that you were a slave in the land of Egypt, and the LORD your God brought you out of there by a mighty hand and by an outstretched arm; therefore the LORD your God commanded you to observe the sabbath day." Thus, the Sabbath became a celebration of freedom as well as a day of rest.

The rest prescribed on the Sabbath is both a physical ceasing of labor and an invitation to receive spiritual refreshment.

In the New Testament, Rabbi Yeshua invites those who are "weary and burdened" to come to Him for rest (Matt. 11:28, NIV). Furthermore, He identified Himself as the "Lord of the Sabbath" (Luke 6:5) and taught that "the Sabbath was made for man and not man for the Sabbath" (Mark 2:27). Through the practice of taking a day a week to receive from the Spirit of Elohim, we receive the very rest of God Himself, who is by His very nature rest. Through Messiah, who released us from the debt and bondages of sin, we have access to this divine refreshment.

Leviticus 23 goes on to address seven feasts, four in the spring and three in the fall. **Passover**, the first of the spring holy days, commemorates how the Lord used the blood of a Passover lamb to deliver the Israelites out of bondage in Egypt. Each family was to take the blood of an unblemished lamb and apply that blood on the doorpost of their home. When the angel of death, which was God's judgment, passed through Egypt that fateful night, the judgment passed over every home that had been marked by the blood of the lamb.

As followers of The Way, we understand that Yeshua is "the Lamb of God who takes away the sin of the world" (John 1:29).

Messiah's death and resurrection fulfill the symbolism of the Passover lamb, providing redemption and freedom from the bondage of sin. Therefore, Passover serves as a powerful reminder of God's salvation through Yeshua. This is why Paul says Christ has become our Passover (1 Cor. 5:7).

During **the Feast of Unleavened Bread**, which begins the day after Passover, Jewish families remove all leaven from their homes and eat only unleavened bread, called matzo. This is done in remembrance of when the children of Israel had to leave Egypt in haste after God instructed them, "When you hear My voice, leave *in haste and do not wait for the bread to rise.*" (See Deuteronomy 16:3.) They were to instantly obey and move out. Thus, the Feast of Unleavened Bread speaks of instantaneous and full obedience.

This is why Jesus' sinless body—symbolized by unleavened bread, free from the leaven of pride—was buried during the Feast of Unleavened Bread. Yeshua is the absolute fulfillment of this holy day, the One who perfectly and immediately obeys the Father. The Feast of Unleavened Bread retains its original meaning for Israel and the Jewish people but took on its fullest and final meaning when Yeshua Himself, the Bread of Heaven, was broken, buried, and given unto us (Luke 22:19).

During **the Feast of Firstfruits**, each individual farmer was to bring the first sheaf of the spring harvest to the priest, who would then lift it up and wave it before the Lord. Yahweh would then deem the farmer's entire harvest acceptable and dedicated to Him.

Consider again that this feast corresponds with the first fruit of the spring harvest. In the winter the sky is often gray and cloudy. There are no leaves on the trees, no splashes of green, no flowers or fruit. The ground is brown and truly looks dead. But when the spring comes, when the weather warms up and April showers water the earth, this dead-looking ground is suddenly made alive. The grass is green again, leaves begin to sprout from those dead-looking trees, flowers spring forth, and fruit grows anew. It is like the earth comes back to life from the dead.

This takes on new meaning when we realize that Yeshua was raised from the dead on this holy day. He is the firstfruits of the harvest and "the firstborn of the dead" (Rev. 1:5). He ascended to heaven as "the first fruits of those who have fallen asleep" (1 Cor. 15:20, MEV), heralding the new creation and the promise of our future resurrection. Yeshua is the first in a long line of God's elect who will be raised from the dead to experience His love and presence in heaven forevermore!

Held seven weeks and a day (fifty days) after Passover, **Shavuot**, also known as Pentecost or the Feast of Weeks, was originally an agricultural feast day. But over the years traditional Judaism associated this feast with the day the Lord appeared on Mount Sinai and gave the Israelites His Law. Every year at this time religious Jews renew their acceptance of God's gift, the Torah.

But Scripture tells of a time when the Law and the lawgiver would draw nearer. Jeremiah 31:33 says, "'But this is the covenant which I will make with the house of Israel after those days,' declares the LORD, 'I will put My law within them and on their heart I will write it; and I will be their God, and they shall be My people.'" Ezekiel also anticipated this time when Yahweh would give His people a new heart and put His Spirit within them (Ezek. 36:26). The Law, once written on stone, would become etched in human hearts.

This was fulfilled in Acts 2, where we find 120 of the first believers in Yeshua gathered together in the Upper Room celebrating Shavuot. As they were there recalling once again how Yahweh appeared in fire on top of the mountain and gave Moses His commandments, suddenly He appeared to them again, afresh and anew—up close and personal!

This encounter inaugurated the prophecies of Ezekiel and Jeremiah that the Lord would no longer speak to His people only by the writings on the tablets of stone. Instead, He was fulfilling these prophecies by communicating to His people from His Spirit within them. Thus, for believers in Yeshua, this feast, the last of the spring holy days, symbolizes the empowerment of the indwelling Holy Spirit, who enables us to fulfill God's purposes and bear witness to His truth.

The Feast of Trumpets, the first of the three fall festivals, was marked in ancient Israel by the blowing of the trumpets, or the shofar. In the Torah the blowing of the trumpets often preceded times when God revealed Himself or was about to break in on behalf of His people. In Exodus 19, the first time the Israelites as a nation encountered Yahweh, the Lord announced Himself with the blowing of a trumpet that proceeded out of heaven (vv. 10–20).

For believers in Messiah this feast is a picture of the rapture. When Jesus returns with the blowing of a trumpet from heaven, those who are not prepared to meet Him will tremble in unspeakable fear. But those of us who are ready to see our God will ascend and meet Messiah in the air, just as Moses did when he went up the mountain to meet God after he heard the heavenly shofar blow.

In 1 Thessalonians 4:16–17 Paul writes: "For the Lord Himself will descend from heaven with a shout, with the voice of the archangel and with the trumpet of God, and the dead in Christ will rise first. Then we who are alive and remain will be caught up together with them in the clouds to meet the Lord in the air, and so we shall always be with the Lord." And Paul says elsewhere, "In a moment, in the twinkling of an eye, at the last trumpet; for the trumpet will sound, and the dead will be raised imperishable, and we will be changed" (1 Cor. 15:52).

In both the past and future, the blowing of the shofar announces God's manifest presence. Thus, the Feast of Trumpets calls believers to be alert and ready. The next time God sounds His trumpet from heaven, it will signal Messiah's return. At this time, His glory will be fully manifested to the entire world.

The Day of Atonement (Yom Kippur, which means "the Day

of Covering") follows the Feast of Trumpets. In ancient times, on this holy day the high priest would go into the Holy of Holies, a sacred room where the Ark of the Covenant was kept, and pour the blood of a bull and a goat on top of the Ark of the Covenant, called the Mercy Seat in Hebrews 9:5. When the Lord saw the blood poured out upon the Mercy Seat, He would overlook the sins of His people for a year.

Leviticus 17:11 declares: "For the life of the flesh is in the blood, and I have given it to you on the altar to make atonement for your souls; for it is the *blood* by reason of the life that makes atonement" (emphasis added). Biblically, the Day of Atonement is about the blood that is shed for the forgiveness and covering of sin.

The Lord can only be in covenant with humanity through a blood atonement, for "without shedding of blood there is no forgiveness" (Heb. 9:22). Therefore, for believers in Yeshua, this holy day symbolizes the ultimate atonement made by Messiah, the sinless One whose blood was poured out, opening the way for us to be in covenant relationship with God forever.

In one way, this feast has been fulfilled, insofar as Yeshua's blood has already been shed and we are able to be in fellowship with God now. But there is also a prophetic way that Yom Kippur will find fulfillment in the future—the Jewish people will turn to Messiah Yeshua. Zechariah 12:10 says, "I will pour out on the house of David and on the inhabitants of Jerusalem, the Spirit of grace and of supplication, so that they will look on Me whom they have pierced; and they will mourn for Him, as one mourns for an only son, and they will weep bitterly over Him like the bitter weeping over a firstborn."

When Yeshua returns, He will lift the veil from their eyes! The Book of Revelation foretells this glorious event that Zechariah wrote about: "Behold, He is coming with the clouds, and every eye will see Him, even those who pierced Him; and all the tribes of the earth will mourn over Him. So it is to be. Amen" (Rev.

1:7). Paul also foretells of this event in Romans 11, stating that at Messiah's return "all Israel will be saved; just as it is written, 'The Deliverer will come from Zion, He will remove ungodliness from Jacob. This is My covenant with them, when I take away their sins'" (vv. 26–27).

The Hebrew Scriptures and the New Testament alike anticipate a time in the future when a mass of Jewish people will receive Yeshua as their Messiah. As they do, the kingdom of God will be fully inaugurated in the earth and the fullness of the Day of Atonement will be gloriously manifest.

Finally, **the Feast of Tabernacles**, or Sukkot, commemorates God's provision and protection during the Israelites' journey through the wilderness. During this feast, at many Jewish homes and synagogues a sukkah—meaning a tabernacle or booth—is built out of lumber, grass, or any other natural substance and serves as a temporary structure reminding Jewish people of the temporary tents the Israelites lived in during their journey toward the Promised Land. It is then decorated with natural materials such as tree branches, leaves, flowers, vegetables, and fruit. Many people will eat their meals and sleep in the sukkah for the entire seven days of the feast, remembering how the Israelites had nothing but God in their forty years of wandering in the wilderness after coming out of Egypt.

For believers in Messiah, Sukkot is a beautiful foreshadowing of how we should live today—totally dependent on God and joyously thankful for His provision. It is also a reminder that just as the Lord was with His people during their wilderness journey—His presence was seen every day for forty years as a pillar of fire by night and a glory cloud hovering over the Tabernacle by day—so is God's presence with us today wherever we go.

The Feast of Tabernacles will find its ultimate fulfillment when Yeshua reigns in the new heaven and the new earth, tabernacling with His people in the fullest sense. (See Revelation 21.)

For believers Sukkot serves as a reminder of the hope of eternal life and the ultimate establishment of God's kingdom.

To recap how Yeshua fulfilled God's spring holy days: He died for us on Passover, was buried on the Feast of Unleavened Bread, rose on the Feast of Firstfruits, and sent the Holy Spirit on Shavuot. Regarding God's fall holy days: Yeshua returns on the Feast of Trumpets, the salvation of Israel is represented in the Day of Atonement, and the Feast of Tabernacles points to the coming new heavens and new earth, where we will forever tabernacle with Messiah.

While believers in Yeshua are not bound by the Levitical Law to observe these feasts, recognizing their significance and what they symbolize can enhance our appreciation of the gospel and the overarching message of Scripture.

Paul wrote in Romans 11:24 and Ephesians 2:12 that Gentile believers have been grafted in to the commonwealth of Israel. Therefore, all of us, Jew and Gentile alike, who are in relationship with Yahweh through Messiah have been grafted into Israel, the olive tree, and, therefore, these holy and appointed days are now an opportunity for spiritual blessing for all God's people!

By remembering the precept to celebrate and honor God's feasts (Lev. 23:2), we are established in faith.

TO BE THANKFUL AND REJOICE ON SUKKOT

Now on the first day you shall take for yourselves the foliage of beautiful trees, palm branches and boughs of leafy trees and willows of the brook, and you shall *rejoice* before the LORD your God for seven days.
—LEVITICUS 23:40, EMPHASIS ADDED

THIS COMMANDMENT HIGHLIGHTS the call to rejoice during the Feast of Tabernacles, also known as Sukkot, which as we have seen is a time of joyous reflection on God's provision and protection during the Israelites' forty-year journey in the wilderness.

While Sukkot is explicitly a season of rejoicing, the charge to rejoice and be grateful in Yahweh is a common theme throughout the Torah. In Deuteronomy 12:7 the Lord instructed Israel that when they were living in the Promised Land they were to "rejoice in all [their] undertakings in which the LORD [their] God has blessed [them]." Elsewhere, Elohim (the Creator) commanded:

> And you shall *rejoice* before the LORD your God, you and your sons and daughters, your male and female servants, and the Levite who is within your gates.
> —DEUTERONOMY 12:12, EMPHASIS ADDED

> You may spend the money for whatever your heart desires... and there you shall eat in the presence of the LORD your God

> and *rejoice*, you and your household.
>
> —DEUTERONOMY 14:26, EMPHASIS ADDED

These scriptures illustrate how important it is to cultivate an attitude of rejoicing as a habit if we are to walk in true fellowship with God's Spirit. Yet the command to rejoice is perhaps most prominently emphasized in relation to Sukkot:

> You shall celebrate the Feast of Booths [Tabernacles] seven days after you have gathered in from your threshing floor and your wine vat; and you shall rejoice in your feast, you and your son and your daughter and your male and female servants and the Levite and the stranger and the orphan and the widow who are in your towns.
>
> —DEUTERONOMY 16:13–14, EMPHASIS ADDED

This festive atmosphere of the Feast of Tabernacles is intended to cultivate gratitude and combat murmuring and complaining, which are great sins that caused God's wrath to fall on Israel.

> So all these curses shall come on you and pursue you and overtake you until you are destroyed....Because you did not serve *the LORD your God with joy and a glad heart*, for the abundance of all things; therefore you shall serve your enemies whom the LORD will send against you, in hunger, in thirst, in nakedness, and in the lack of all things; and He will put an iron yoke on your neck until He has destroyed you.
>
> —DEUTERONOMY 28:45, 47–48, EMPHASIS ADDED

We must realize it is actually a sin to walk in the spirit of entitlement, and fight against it by cultivating a spirit of joy and thankfulness.

In the New Testament we see that Yeshua celebrated Sukkot, and we read that on the last day of the feast Messiah cried out, "If anyone is thirsty, let him come to Me and drink. He who believes in Me, as the Scripture said, 'From his innermost being will flow rivers of living water [the Holy Spirit]'" (John 7:37–38).

For believers, Jew and Gentile alike, Sukkot is a powerful, annual reminder to nurture gratitude by recognizing all that God has provided and blessed us with spiritually, materially, and relationally. In a world where discontent, complaining, and entitlement often dominate, the command to be thankful and rejoice on Sukkot (Lev. 23:40) calls us to overcome and transcend the darkness by willfully choosing to be grateful and in so doing enter God's holy joy and light.

TO CELEBRATE THE YEAR OF JUBILEE EVERY FIFTIETH YEAR

You shall thus consecrate the fiftieth year and proclaim a release through the land to all its inhabitants. It shall be a jubilee for you, and each of you shall return to his own property, and each of you shall return to his family.
—Leviticus 25:10

We previously covered the Shemitah, or sabbatical year, which happens every seven years. Now we turn our attention to the Year of Jubilee, which occurred every fifty years as a time of liberation and socioeconomic refresh in ancient Israel. Slaves were freed, debts were forgiven, and lands were returned to their original owners.

Consider that the Jubilee happened every fiftieth year and the number fifty comes after seven cycles of seven. One source makes this observation:

> The number 50 is the distinguished number of transcendence. The count up to 50 is composed of two essential and distinct stages. The first phase is the step-by-step progression rising from 1 up to 49. As the square of 7 ($7^2 = 49$), 49 denotes the complete cycle within the physical universe. This is a natural development, one that reaches the extremities of the outer boundaries. This may be the furthest limit as far as nature is concerned—but it is not the endpoint. But the ultimate destination of a Jew is his arrival at the second phase—one where

> he somehow manages the supernatural leap from 49 to arrive at the transcendental quality of 50.[16]

This quote, taken from Rabbinic Judaism, points out that the natural cycle of creation is seven days, and every week we start over walking out that natural cycle of seven. Similarly in the Torah, every seventh year is a sabbatical year. But consider that in mystical Judaism, the number of eternity and infinity is not seven but eight. (This is why Jewish males are circumcised on the eighth day.) The idea of the Year of Jubilee is that after living locked in to the natural order of seven, Yahweh breaks in and delivers us into eternity through Yeshua the Messiah, who is the fulfillment of the Year of Jubilee. Messiah even began His ministry by reading from Isaiah 61:1–2, declaring that He had come "to proclaim liberty to captives and freedom to prisoners" (v. 1), which points to the Jubilee year.

This law to celebrate the Jubilee year flows from God's desire for justice, mercy, and equality among His people, and it teaches us that God is the ultimate owner of all things and we are merely stewards of His creation.

Psalm 24:1 declares, "The earth is the LORD's, and everything in it" (NIV). Property changes hands from one owner to the next as it is bought and sold, but ultimately the property belongs to the Creator. To say it another way, it is not we who own the land. We may possess the deed for a few years, but God, the Holy One, owns the world. This perspective helps us hold possessions loosely, understanding that our ultimate treasure is in heaven (Matt. 6:19–21).

Also during the Jubilee year, an Israelite who had sold himself was able to return to his own family and property and be restored.

> If a countryman of yours becomes so poor with regard to you that he sells himself to you, you shall not subject him to a slave's service. He shall be with you as a hired man, as if he were a sojourner; he shall serve with you until the year of

> jubilee. He shall then go out from you, he and his sons with him, and shall go back to his family, that he may return to the property of his forefathers. For they are My servants whom I brought out from the land of Egypt; they are not to be sold in a slave sale.
>
> —Leviticus 25:39–42

The return of Israelites to their own families and properties kept the tribes of Israel intact until the coming of Messiah. In other words, families that had been separated for economic reasons were reunited, thereby preserving the pure bloodlines of each tribe. So we can be assured that Messiah Jesus was truly from the tribe of Judah because the family lines had been kept intact through the laws of the Jubilee year.

The principles of the Jubilee year are also evident in the United States, pointing to the nation's Judeo-Christian heritage. In fact, Leviticus 25:10 (KJV) is inscribed on the Liberty Bell in Philadelphia: "Proclaim liberty throughout all the land unto all the inhabitants thereof." The aspiration for freedom, liberty, and happiness that reflect the themes of the Jubilee year is also ingrained in the United States' Declaration of Independence: "We hold these truths to be self-evident, that all men are created equal, that they are endowed by their Creator with certain unalienable Rights, that among these are Life, Liberty and the pursuit of Happiness."

Finally, as it highlighted freedom, the Year of Jubilee mandated the forgiveness of debts. This calls us to generosity and mercy. Yeshua modeled this in its most expansive form—He canceled and released us from the record of debt that stood against us. As Revelation 1:5 says, He "*released* us from our sins" (emphasis added). Freely we have been forgiven, so freely we must give and forgive. May the command to celebrate the Year of Jubilee (Lev. 25:10) inspire us to live in the enormity of God's heart that this holy year reveals.

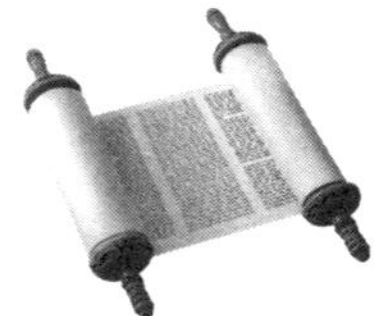

ONCE WE DEDICATE SOMETHING TO GOD, WE HAVE NO RIGHT TO TAKE IT BACK

Anything which a man sets apart to the LORD out of
all that he has...shall not be sold or redeemed.
—LEVITICUS 27:28

THE TORAH REVEALS that once an offering is dedicated and released to Elohim, that which was offered to Him now transcends human ownership, and we no longer have rights to it. Therefore, we can't take it back.

In this mitzvah, we see the need to be people of our word. At the congregation I led for many years, there were times when people requested the return of their offerings. Sometimes they were angry about something I said. Other times they needed the resources back to meet a personal need. Both situations highlight how difficult it can be to truly relinquish what we have offered to God once and for all.

We may have the same challenge in our spiritual commitments. Some of us may, in moments of great zeal for the Lord, dedicate our time or resources to Him, only to later retract those promises.

We see a positive example of dedication in Yeshua's calling of the disciples. When Messiah invited them to follow Him, the disciples left their livelihoods without looking back (Matt. 4:18–22). Their decision was final, and there was no returning to their old lives. Some of the disciples temporarily returned to fishing after Yeshua's crucifixion but then came back to wholeheartedly serve Him with full commitment (John 21:1–14).

Our dedication to God can take many forms. We can devote our talents, careers, or time to serving Him. When we do so, we must keep in mind this command informing us that once we dedicate something to God, we are not to take it back (Lev. 27:28). Our commitments are sacred, and failing to fulfill them undermines the act of worship our dedications represent.

TO HONOR GOD WITH OUR TITHES

Thus all the tithe of the land, of the seed of the land or of the fruit of the tree, is the LORD's; it is holy to the LORD.
—LEVITICUS 27:30

THE COMMAND TO tithe reflects a fundamental principle in the Torah: Everything belongs to God. The Israelites were instructed to set aside a tenth (a tithe) of their produce—whether from the yield of the land or the fruit of the trees—as holy to the Lord. This act of giving was not merely a ritual but an acknowledgment that Adon Olam (the Master of the Universe) owns everything. It caused the Israelites to remember that their blessings, including the land they cultivated, were gifts from God. The tithe also supported the Levites, who served in the Temple.

The command to tithe has at times been used to manipulate people, and as a result some immediately close their ears when the subject is broached. But the reality is that tithing is a very important subject. If we're not surrendered to God in the area of our finances, we're not fully surrendered to Him.

We often tend to trust in our finances for security. When we surrender our monetary resources to the Lord by tithing our income with pure *kavanah* (the Hebrew word for *intention*), we're saying, "Lord, I'm going to trust in You. You, not my finances, are the source of my security." Tithing is not about legalism; it is an act of honor, trust, and love. In fact, tithing demonstrates a holy fear of the Lord, which Deuteronomy 14:22–23 reveals: "You shall surely tithe...so that you may learn to fear the LORD your God always."

The precept of tithing predates the Law. It is first seen in the Book of Genesis when Abraham gave a tenth of all he had to the priest Melchizedek. Yeshua affirmed its practice when He addressed the Pharisees in Matthew 23:23, saying, "Woe to you, teachers of the law and Pharisees, you hypocrites! You give a tenth of your spices—mint, dill, and cumin. But you have neglected the more important matters of the law—justice, mercy and faithfulness. You should have practiced the latter, without neglecting the former" (NIV). Yeshua's point was that our offerings should come from a place of genuine love for God rather than mere rule-compliance. Paul similarly addressed this: "Each of you should give what you have decided in your heart to give, not reluctantly or under compulsion, for God loves a cheerful giver" (2 Cor. 9:7, NIV).

When we surrender to God in the area of our finances, we open our hearts for Him to pour back into it. Malachi 3:10 says, "'Bring the whole tithe into the storehouse, so that there may be food in My house, and test Me now in this,' says the LORD of hosts, 'if I will not open for you the windows of heaven and pour out for you a blessing until it overflows.'"

Even as Israel was commanded to honor the Creator with their tithes (Lev. 27:30) and was promised to receive a blessing as a result, so too is the case for us today. Tithing is an act of worship that reflects a heart of gratitude and a commitment to reverencing God. It is a physical expression of our trust in His promises and care for our well-being.

TO SEND THE RITUALLY UNCLEAN OUTSIDE THE CAMP

Command the sons of Israel that they send away from the camp every leper and everyone having a discharge and everyone who is unclean because of a dead person. You shall send away both male and female; you shall send them outside the camp so that they will not defile their camp where I dwell in their midst.
—Numbers 5:2–3

In the ancient Israelite camp, God's Shekinah glory—His divine presence—rested among His people. The camp was a holy place, and maintaining its purity was essential for the people to remain in fellowship with the Holy One of Israel and dwell in harmony with Him. Thus, those who were ritually unclean, whether due to leprosy, bodily discharges, or contact with a dead body, had to be sent outside the community.

The principle to send the unclean out of the camp highlights God's purity and the seriousness of sin, and it remains in place in the New Covenant (New Testament). Addressing the issue of moral and spiritual impurity within the body of believers, Paul writes: "Remove the wicked man from among yourselves" (1 Cor. 5:13).

Tolerating uncleanness or immorality weakens a congregation. Compromise drains people of their resolve to obey God and dilutes holiness. It changes the whole culture of the assembly of the elect. I am convinced that loose standards of dress have fostered a culture where fornication, adultery, and sexual immorality have increased—because we did not define standards well enough or discipline people who would not abide by them.

A correction is needed to our present culture, where many are run by their emotions rather than the truth. Like parents who do not discipline their children and as a result end up with an atmosphere of chaos and rebellion in their homes, so too will the body of Messiah be when impurity is not dealt with.

The command to send the ritually unclean outside the camp to prevent defilement (Num. 5:2–3) is a reminder that we must be vigilant to safeguard our lives and our spiritual communities from moral and spiritual corruption. This is why Rabbi Shaul (Paul) warns, "A little leaven leavens the whole lump of dough" (Gal. 5:9).

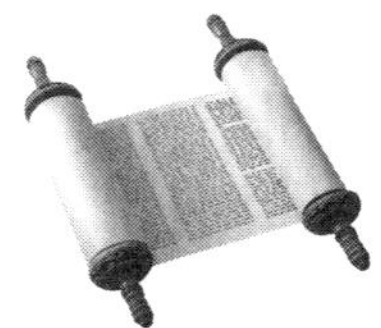

TO CONFESS ONE'S SIN

Speak to the sons of Israel, "When a man or woman commits any of the sins of mankind, acting unfaithfully against the LORD, and that person is guilty, then he shall confess his sins which he has committed."
—NUMBERS 5:6–7

CONFESSION—BRINGING OUR TRANSGRESSIONS into the light—is a cornerstone of Torah wisdom. In the Hebrew Bible confession is not merely an admission of wrongdoing; it is to be accompanied by genuine remorse and a commitment to restitution. Confession is the first step in a journey of repentance and restoration. In Hebrew, the act of returning to the Lord is called *teshuvah.*

The fact that along with confession restitution was required (Num. 5:7–8) illustrates that we are not talking about light confession, mumbling a half-hearted "I'm sorry" and then moving on without thinking about it again and being transformed. Rather, it involves an attitude of remorse and commitment to not commit the sin again. *Teshuvah* means resolutely turning away from our sin unto the Lord. True repentance takes place when there is a change of heart evidenced by actions that reflect our commitment to God.

The ministry of John the Immerser (John the Baptist) exemplifies this commandment. In Matthew 3:6 we read about individuals *confessing their sins* and being baptized as public declarations of repentance. But John's baptism was not a call for a onetime confession but for a life transformed. As he admonished, "Therefore bear fruit in keeping with repentance" (Matt. 3:8). Bearing fruit will follow true, heartfelt confession.

Confession serves as a deterrent against future sin. When we bring our sins into God's light and into others' view when appropriate, we experience the full weight of our shame accompanied by genuine remorse. This process is essential for real repentance, as it creates a strong resolve to turn away from sin. David experienced the freedom true confession brings, as is seen in Psalm 32:5, "I acknowledged my sin to You, and my iniquity I did not hide; I said, 'I will confess my transgressions to the LORD'; and You forgave the guilt of my sin." First John 1:9 assures us, "If we confess our sins, He is faithful and righteous to forgive us our sins and to cleanse us from all unrighteousness."

The commandment to confess our sins (Num. 5:6–7) is deeply rooted in both the Torah and the New Testament. Honest confession is the pathway to cleansing, transformation, light, and wholeness.

THE COMMAND FOR THE PRIESTS TO BLESS ISRAEL

Speak to Aaron and to his sons, saying, "Thus you shall bless the sons of Israel. You shall say to them: The LORD bless you, and keep you; the LORD make His face shine on you, and be gracious to you; the LORD lift up His countenance on you, and give you peace." So they shall invoke My name on the sons of Israel, and I then will bless them.
—NUMBERS 6:23–27

THIS MITZVAH IS known as the Priestly or Aaronic Blessing. But in reality it is not the priests' blessing upon God's people; the blessing originates from Yahweh. The Lord told Aaron and his sons exactly what to say, and each line of this short but powerful blessing reveals what our Maker wants us to know about His love, power, and goodness toward Israel and all His children, Jew and Gentile alike.

"The Lord bless you, and keep you." This speaks of God's provision and protection. The phrase "bless you" comes from the Hebrew term *yevarechecha*, which conveys the sense of a king stooping down and presenting a gift to one of his subjects. This word picture captures the love, favor, and grace God has for His people and reflects His disposition toward us as the One who stooped down to love, bless, and receive us right where we are.

The term "keep you" comes from the Hebrew *veyishmerecha*, which paints a picture of a kind shepherd corralling his sheep to protect them. This part of the blessing reminds us that though we live in a world full of dangers all around, we can be confident that the Lord is protecting and keeping us.

"The Lord make His face shine on you, and be gracious to you." God's face is toward His people, and He is looking at us with eyes of love, extending His grace to us. His strength, glory, and goodness are all being directed toward us.

The word translated "gracious" in this passage is *vichunekka*, which carries the idea, once again, of a king stooping down in mercy and tenderness toward an inferior. Think about it: God, who could smash us with His fist and annihilate us if He wanted to, instead chooses to be kind to us, though we have no claim to His benevolence and have done nothing to deserve it. This is what Yeshua, the Word, did for you and me when He became a man, clothing Himself in flesh and blood and dying on the cross. He stooped down to forgive and remove our sin because He loves us and wants to be in relationship with us.

"The Lord lift up His countenance on you, and give you peace." The first part of this statement—"The Lord lift up His countenance on you"—communicates the idea of a father lifting up his baby and beaming as he gazes at his child. It's hard for many of us to believe, but this is how God feels about you and me. He enjoys and delights in us. To "lift up His countenance" on us is to bring us into His heart. He wants to fellowship with you and me.

Finally, through the intimacy of knowing God, we find peace. As you may know, the Hebrew word for *peace* is *shalom*. Shalom is not just the absence of conflict; it means complete wholeness—spirit, soul, mind, and body. This is what God purposes and desires for us. Paul wrote in Colossians 2:10, "In Him [Yeshua] you have been made complete." The gift God has given us through Messiah is His own completeness, His own shalom.

The Aaronic Blessing is not a ritualistic formula or a poetic pleasantry. This prayer comes from the essence of God's heart.

It is a living declaration of God's disposition toward His people, and He wants us to walk confidently in it.

As I said previously, Gentile believers have been grafted into the commonwealth of Israel. If you are a follower of Yeshua, you are one of God's elect. His chosen ones extend beyond the physical descendants of Abraham, Isaac, and Jacob. This prayer is for you. The blessing God spoke over ancient Israel (Num. 6:23–27) He speaks over your life today.

And as the ancient priests were commanded to speak this blessing over the Israelites, so are we to declare it over others. In Yeshua, all believers belong to a "royal priesthood" (1 Pet. 2:9), and we are empowered to pronounce blessings on others. The New Testament writings tell us, "You also...are being built up as...a holy priesthood" (1 Pet. 2:5), and "He has made us to be a kingdom, priests to His God and Father" (Rev. 1:6).

These scriptures express our identity and role as priests. Just as the priests in Numbers were commanded to bless the people of Israel, we too can and should by the leading of God's Spirit invoke His blessings upon others. But we must remember that ultimately only Yahweh has the power to bless. Therefore, we should say, "May God bless you," not, "I bless you."

Because we are God's priests, our prayers and blessings carry divine authority when they align with God's will. As we consider the command for the priests to bless Israel (Num. 6:23–27), may it be for us a powerful revelation and reminder of how our Maker sees and loves us.

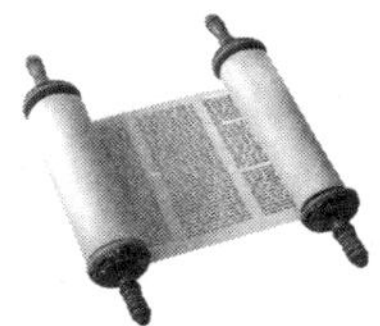

TO BLOW THE TRUMPETS

When you go to war in your land against the adversary who attacks you, then you shall sound an alarm with the trumpets, that you may be remembered before the LORD your God, and be saved from your enemies. Also in the day of your gladness and in your appointed feasts, and on the first days of your months, you shall blow the trumpets over your burnt offerings, and over the sacrifices of your peace offerings; and they shall be as a reminder of you before your God. I am the LORD your God.

—NUMBERS 10:9–10

THE ISRAELITES WERE instructed to sound trumpets in various circumstances: before going to war, during times of joy, on feast days, at the beginning of each month, and over their offerings and sacrifices. These trumpets arrested people's attention, unified the congregation, and signaled important events with their blasts.

Psalm 81:3–4 (ESV) says, "Blow the trumpet at the new moon, at the full moon, on our feast day. For it is a statute for Israel, a rule of the God of Jacob." Joel 2:1 (ESV) declares, "Blow a trumpet in Zion; sound an alarm on my holy mountain! Let all the inhabitants of the land tremble, for the day of the LORD is coming; it is near." These passages highlight the trumpet's role in signaling significant events and calling the community to action.

And the sounding of the trumpet carries even greater spiritual significance. When God revealed Himself to the Israelites on Mount Sinai, "there were thunder and lightning flashes and a thick cloud upon the mountain and a very loud trumpet sound, so that all the people who were in the camp trembled" (Exod. 19:16). This was a prophetic event whose fulfillment the Bible commands us to eagerly anticipate, as it points to the future sounding of a trumpet that will announce Yeshua's return (1 Thess. 4:16). This will mark the culmination of God's redemptive plan in this age when heaven and earth collide, ushering in His eternal kingdom.

Consider also that the sounding of the trumpet pierces through all other noises and causes the hearer to focus his attention on its sound. The command to blow the trumpets, then, is a call to keep our focus (*kavanah*) on the Holy and Blessed One. We are to rise above all earthly and worldly distractions to maintain our *kavanah* on the Lord.

Thus, this precept to blow the trumpets (Num. 10:9–10) reminds us to live in a posture of focused commitment to God and purposeful expectation of Messiah's return as we pursue a deeper relationship with Adonai and proclaim His goodness in the earth.

TO WEAR THE TZITZIT AND TEFILLIN

> Speak to the sons of Israel, and tell them that they shall make for themselves tassels on the corners of their garments throughout their generations, and that they shall put on the tassel of each corner a cord of blue. It shall be a tassel for you to look at and remember all the commandments of the LORD, so as to do them and not follow after your own heart and your own eyes, after which you played the harlot.
>
> —NUMBERS 15:38–39

THE CHILDREN OF Israel, like all humanity, were prone to wander into idolatry and immorality. We read in the writings of the Hebrew prophets that Israel often went astray, following after the lusts of their hearts and eyes. They forsook God's commandments and fell into spiritual adultery. The tzitzit, or tassels, and the tefillin, also known as phylacteries, were given to Israel by the Lord to remind them of His commandments so they would not sin but instead live according to the Torah.

The tzitzit are rich with symbolism. They were to be worn "on the corners of their garments throughout their generations" (Num. 15:38). Since contemporary shirts do not have distinct corners but are generally rounded, and T-shirts have no corners at all, the four-cornered Jewish prayer shawl, called a tallit in Hebrew, and the tallit katan, a four-cornered garment worn underneath the shirt, were made specifically for wearing the tassels. The prayer shawl and tallit katan are not sacred, only the tzitzit (tassels) that hang from their corners.

According to Rabbinic Judaism, the garment the tzitzit hangs from needs four corners to express the four aspects of redemption the Israelites received when God delivered them out of Egypt. To put it another way, the four corners "correspond to the four expressions of redemption associated with the Exodus"[17]:

> I am the LORD, and *I will bring you out* from under the burdens of the Egyptians, and *I will deliver you* from their bondage. *I will also redeem you* with an outstretched arm and with great judgments. Then *I will take you* for My people, and I will be your God.
>
> —EXODUS 6:6–7, EMPHASIS ADDED

But not only do the four corners of the garment connect us to the past redemption out of Egypt; they point to our future redemption as well. According to Rabbinic tradition, "In the messianic era G-d will gather us from the 'four corners (*kanfot*) of the world,' corresponding to the four corners of the *tallit*."[18] This is confirmed by Rabbi Yeshua's words in Matthew 24:31, "The great trumpet will sound, and he will send out his angels to the four corners of the earth, and they will gather his chosen people from one end of the world to the other" (GNT). Thus, we see that the tzitzit, worn on the four corners of the garment, point to the Creator's sovereignty over the entire earth.

Although most prayer shawls today do not include a blue tassel, they should. The commandment states that hanging from each corner of the garment was to be "a cord of blue." I won't get into the reasons most modern prayer shawls do not contain a cord of blue other than to say it is a case of "straining out a gnat and swallowing a camel" (Matt. 23:24).[19]

The dyed blue cord, derived from a rare sea creature, speaks of divinity and the presence of God. Blue is a reminder of the sea, sky, and heavens, whose heights and depths seem to go on forever. It speaks to us of God's transcendence—that He's always looking down on His creation in love and understands everything going on in the world and in our lives.

In the Tabernacle, where God dwelled with His people, the Ark of the Covenant, Table of Showbread, Golden Lampstands, Altar of Incense, and all the articles used for ministry were covered in blue (Num. 4:5–11). This special color reminds us that we can't escape God. Blue calls us to look up and remember the source of our lives.

Before moving on to the tefillin, or phylacteries (Deut. 6:8), I want to address one more interesting point about the tzitzit that I mentioned in the introduction. According to Rabbinic Judaism, the numerical value of the tzitzit is 613, corresponding to the 613 laws of the Torah. Every letter in the Hebrew alphabet has a corresponding numerical value, and Rashi, one of Judaism's most famous Torah commentators, calculated that the five letters that comprise the word *tzitzit* add up to 600. When you add 600 to the eight threads and five knots of each tassel, the total is 613, making the tzitzit a constant reminder of God's 613 commandments.

Now, regarding the tefillin, these are small black leather boxes containing scrolls of parchment inscribed with Torah texts. These boxes are bound to the arm and forehead during weekday morning prayers. The tefillin are a physical reminder of the spiritual truths of the Torah that should guide our actions (arm) and thoughts (forehead).

Wearing tefillin on the arm symbolizes a person's commitment to act according to God's commandments. Placing it on the forehead signifies a person's dedication to keeping their mind focused on HaShem and His Word. This dual symbolism reinforces the complete nature of devotion, involving both thoughts and actions. It is as Psalm 119:11 says: "I have hidden your word in my heart that I might not sin against you" (NIV).

The purpose of the tefillin, once again, is that daily one

would have a visible reminder to keep focused on walking in God's ways. Unfortunately, in the New Testament, we see that this mitzvah, intended to keep the Lord's servants focused on Him, morphed into an unholy religious status symbol. Yeshua rebuked the Pharisees for broadening their phylacteries (tefillin) and lengthening their tassels (tzitzit), not to remind themselves to obey God's commandments but rather to be looked upon as pious by others. They were doing it, Rabbi Jesus said, "to be noticed by men" (Matt. 23:5).

Wearing the tzitzit and tefillin is a way of practicing mindfulness, reminding us of the Torah's commandments and encouraging us to live righteously. In contemporary times the wearing of tzitzit and tefillin is much like the practice among some followers of Yeshua of wearing bracelets or other items inscribed with "What Would Jesus Do?" or similar slogans that serve to remind the wearer that they are under God's lordship.

The goal of the tzitzit and tefillin is to remind us to stay focused every day and not open our thoughts or hearts to that which opposes the kingdom of God. Father once said to me, "Seize My Word and don't let anything else in." We must cut off thinking and desires that are evil in origin no matter how much our hearts desire them or our eyes lust after them. John the apostle urged us, "Do not love the world....For all that is in the world, the lust of the flesh and the lust of the eyes and the boastful pride of life, is not from the Father, but is from the world" (1 John 2:15–16).

Consider the tenth commandment: "You shall not covet your neighbor's house; you shall not covet your neighbor's wife or his male servant or his female servant or his ox or his donkey or anything that belongs to your neighbor" (Exod. 20:17). How much less jealousy, adultery, and destruction would there be if we quickly cut off thoughts of wanting to take what is not ours and instead redirected ourselves to be at peace with God and what we have? This is why in connection with the tzitzit, Numbers

15:39 warns not to go after the cravings of our eyes. When a Jew looks down at the tassels hanging from the four corners of their garment, they are reminded to turn their eyes away from lust. Whether we are literally wearing the tassels or not, taking the warnings in the Torah seriously will guard us from falling.

The pure goal of this mitzvah is that each time a Jewish person sees the tzitzit or the tefillin, they think of their commitment to God and His ways. This command to wear them (Num. 15:38–39) calls us as New Covenant believers to anchor ourselves in God's Word and stay focused on it so we are not led astray by our own desires or the subtle influences of the world.

TO OFFER THE LORD A LAMB EVERY DAY IN THE MORNING AND EVENING

Then the LORD spoke to Moses, saying, "Command the sons of Israel and say to them, 'You shall be careful to present My offering, *My food* for My offerings by *fire*, of a *soothing aroma* to Me, at their appointed time.' You shall say to them, 'This is the offering by fire which you shall offer to the LORD: *two male lambs one year old without defect as a continual burnt offering every day. You shall offer the one lamb in the morning and the other lamb you shall offer at twilight.*'"
—NUMBERS 28:1–4, EMPHASIS ADDED

THE HEBREW WORD for *offering* in this passage is *olah*, which means that which ascends and goes up in smoke. What a powerful picture of worship. The ascending smoke from the offerings illustrates that the souls of God's elect should be reaching upward to the Lord.

The offerings by fire of two male lambs, each a year old and without defect, were to be presented as a continual burnt offering every day, one in the morning and the other at twilight. The timing of the offerings—at dawn and twilight—highlights God's provision and mercy, which are new every morning and extend through the night. This is why the psalmist declared, "It is good to give thanks to the LORD and to sing praises to Your name, O Most High; to declare Your lovingkindness in the morning and Your faithfulness by night" (Ps. 92:1–2).

This mitzvah paints a picture of the call for Israel and God's people today to walk in a posture of 24/7 worship and allegiance to HaShem. These burnt offerings were entirely consumed by the fire, and their smoke ascended into the sky and disappeared, an image of a life that is 100 percent consumed by passion for God.

In ancient Israel the morning sacrifice was given when the first light appeared in the east. Similarly, beginning our days with prayer and reflection sets the tone for the rest of our day, helping us to choose actions and thoughts that please our Savior.

The ancient Israelites offered the evening sacrifice as the shadows began to fall. For followers of The Way, the evening sacrifice signifies the end of our day and a time to reflect on God's faithfulness. We commit ourselves to Him as we enter our rest, "for He gives to His beloved even in his sleep" (Ps. 127:2). When we are unconscious and asleep at night, we are spiritually vulnerable, but, Baruch HaShem, through and in Messiah Jesus, God's *shekinah* glory is always covering our lives—when we are asleep and when we are awake, yesterday, today, and forever.

Here is one more thought to consider: Even as we humans need food each day, so also the children of Israel were required to continually offer up to the Lord the lambs, which this mitzvah calls God's food: "You shall be careful to present My offering, My food" (Num. 28:2). Somehow our willingly offering ourselves up to the Father fulfills Him. Amazingly, our intentional love and obedience are *His food*.

The priests were *continually* engaged in the activity of offering up their sacrifices and as a result were constantly stirred to offer their lives unto God as living sacrifices. Night and day they were occupied with service to their Lord. Their offerings became unto Him a "soothing aroma." When we give our entire lives to God, it satisfies His longing and will for our lives.

Honoring the command to offer the Lord a lamb every day

in the morning and evening (Num. 28:1–4) resulted in Yahweh's presence abiding with them. Similarly, as we consecrate our hearts to Father, the companionship of the Comforter will rest upon our lives. The fellowship of the Blessed One through His Spirit is of ultimate value, surpassing any material possession or worldly status we attain.

THE COMMAND TO NOT BREAK OUR WORD

If a man makes a *vow* to the LORD, or takes an *oath* to bind himself with a binding obligation, he shall not violate his word; he shall do according to all that proceeds out of his mouth.
—NUMBERS 30:2, EMPHASIS ADDED

THE DISTINCTION BETWEEN an oath and a vow is somewhat technical, as one source explains: A vow is tied to an object—when a person prohibits something to themselves, like wine or sex, the vow applies to that specific thing. An oath, on the other hand, is tied to the person—it involves swearing that one will perform a particular action or attesting that something is true.[20]

Both vows and oaths are seen as serious matters in Jewish tradition. Although the Bible includes examples of individuals making vows, by the rabbinic period (AD 70–AD 600) the practice was strongly discouraged. The Shulchan Aruch explicitly advises against making vows frequently, and states that even if someone fulfills a vow, they are still regarded as sinful. To avoid this, "many observant Jews have the practice of saying b'li neder ('without a vow')" to indicate that they are making a commitment or promise but without it having the formal status of being a vow.[21]

Rabbi Yeshua similarly taught, "Again, you have heard that the ancients were told, 'You shall not make false vows, but shall fulfill your vows to the Lord.' But I say to you, make no oath at all, either by heaven, for it is the throne of God, or by the earth, for it is the footstool of His feet, or by Jerusalem, for it is the city of the great King. Nor shall you make an oath by your head, for you cannot make one hair white or black. But let your statement be, 'Yes, yes' or 'No, no'; anything beyond these is of evil" (Matt. 5:33–37). We cannot disconnect Jesus from His Jewishness. He was called "rabbi" (Mark 9:5; 11:21), and much of His teaching reflected the rabbinic thought of His day.

Vows and oaths are not necessary when we are duty bound to keep our word. Our words must be straight, true, stable, and trustworthy. What we say we will do, we must do. This applies to what we speak both to God and to others.

How many times have we given someone our word and then broken it? Maybe we say, "I won't do this again," but we do. Or perhaps a friend tells us something in confidence and we promise not to share it, then find ourselves repeating it to someone else with the plea, "Don't tell anyone I told you this."

Even more seriously, how many of us have made promises to God and then broken them? We say, "Lord, if You do this, I will do that," and then we don't follow through. God sees this, and our actions matter to Him. Too often we make excuses for our disobedience and say, "Grace covers it." Grace does cover our sin, but there are often consequences for not respecting God and keeping our word to Him. He will chastise us to conform us into the image of His Son. Hebrews 12:6 reminds us that "the Lord disciplines the one he loves, and chastises every son whom he receives" (ESV). We need to feel the weight of what we vow to Him.

Keeping our word is a reflection of our personal integrity. It establishes trust and credibility, both in personal and professional relationships. Once broken, trust is not easily rebuilt, so the importance of keeping our word is a responsibility we must take solemnly.

This command extends beyond verbal promises to include commitments made through written agreements, contracts, and even implied obligations. When we enter into any form of agreement, we must do so with the intention of fulfilling our part faithfully. This principle is universal and exists in nearly all cultures and religions worldwide as a cornerstone of ethical and moral behavior.

The command to not break our word in Numbers 30:2 is reiterated in Deuteronomy 23:23: "You shall be careful to perform what goes out from your lips, just as you have voluntarily vowed to the LORD your God, what you have promised." Words spoken and kept exhibit our character and build trust in all relationships.

TO APPOINT MEN AS JUDGES WHO ARE LEARNED IN THE LAWS OF THE TORAH

So I took the heads of your tribes, wise and experienced men, and appointed them heads over you, leaders of thousands and of hundreds, of fifties and of tens, and officers for your tribes. Then I charged your judges at that time, saying, "Hear the cases between your fellow countrymen, and judge righteously between a man and his fellow countryman, or the alien who is with him. You shall not show partiality in judgment; you shall hear the small and the great alike. You shall not fear man, for the judgment is God's."
—Deuteronomy 1:15–17

While this passage does not explicitly state that judges must be learned in the Torah, Rabbinic Judaism infers that this is implied. The intent of this law was to ensure that judges in Israel were not only wise and experienced but also deeply knowledgeable in the laws of the Pentateuch. This was essential in order to maintain justice within the community. Judges were commanded to hear cases impartially, treating all individuals equally, regardless of their social status, and rendering judgments that reflected God's standards, not human biases or fears.

In order for these judges to administer justice righteously, they had to be knowledgeable in the laws of the Torah. The cases they heard were not only religious in nature but civil as well. This meant that in order to make righteous judgments among Israel's "fellow countrymen" (Deut. 1:16), they needed to be grounded in the precepts of the Torah.

This principle is reinforced by Yeshua's teachings and the New Testament writings, which emphasize that leadership within the body of believers should be based on spiritual qualifications rather than worldly achievements. Too often people are promoted within believing communities because of their status in the secular world. Doctors, lawyers, and wealthy individuals find themselves in positions of authority not always because of their spiritual maturity or knowledge of God's Word but because of their "achievements." This leads to a misalignment of values and priorities within the community of faith.

Spiritually immature leaders more easily cave to cultural pressures. Why, for example, have many denominations affirmed homosexuality as an acceptable lifestyle when it is in violation of scriptural standards? When one is not rooted in God's Word, the fear of man and anxiety over the repercussions of standing against the secular tide prevent him from being a grounded judge.

This is why Paul's instructions to Timothy and Titus about the qualifications for elders and overseers highlight spiritual maturity, moral integrity, and sound doctrine. Leaders should be above reproach, self-controlled, hospitable, able to teach, not given to drunkenness or violence, and holding firmly to the trustworthy message as taught (1 Tim. 3:1–7; Titus 1:5–9). Their lives should be a testament to their faith and commitment to following Yeshua.

Honoring the command to appoint leaders who are well-versed in the Scriptures and who demonstrate godly character (Deut. 1:15–17) helps to ensure that those under their influence will be protected, treated fairly, and remain faithful to God.

THE PRECEPT OF THE ONENESS OF THE ETERNAL LORD

Hear, O Israel! The LORD is our God, the LORD is one!
—DEUTERONOMY 6:4

WE ARE COMMANDED to believe that the eternal Lord, the One who has produced all existence, is the Ruler of all and has no equal. We must actively hear, know, and believe in Him, trusting in His kingship and sovereignty over the world. We read in the Torah, "Know therefore today, and take it to your heart, that the LORD, He is God in heaven above and on the earth below; there is no other" (Deut. 4:39). And the Lord declares in Isaiah 45:6, "There is no one besides Me. I am the LORD, and there is no other."

In addition to declaring that Yahweh alone is the sovereign of the universe and the one and only Lord, Deuteronomy 6:4 also affirms the unity of God. Our experiences of God can vary. For example, sometimes we may encounter Him as fearsome, as the Israelites did when they trembled before the Most High at the base of Mount Sinai:

> So it came about on the third day, when it was morning, that there were thunder and lightning flashes and a thick cloud upon the mountain and a very loud trumpet sound, so that all

> the people who were in the camp *trembled*.
>
> —Exodus 19:16, emphasis added

At other times Adonai makes Himself known as a tenderhearted Father, as David recorded in the Psalms: "Just as a father has compassion on his children, so the Lord has compassion on those who fear Him" (Ps. 103:13).

Solomon brought to light that the eternal One is also mysterious: "Just as you do not know the path of the wind and how bones are formed in the womb of the pregnant woman, so you do not know the activity of God who makes all things" (Eccles. 11:5).

The point is, although God is like a diamond in that He is multidimensional and multifaceted, He is one. Whether we experience His comfort or His stern rebuke, He is still one and the same God.

As we consider the essential unity of God, think about how believers sometimes struggle to see that the God of the Old Testament (the Hebrew Bible, or Tanakh) and the God of the New Testament (the Brit Chadashah) are the same God. To many the God of the Hebrew Bible seems harsh and unmerciful while the God of the New Testament seems kind and compassionate. However, notice what the Lord said about Himself in Exodus 34:6–7 (emphasis added):

> The Lord, the Lord God, compassionate and *gracious*, slow to anger, and *abounding in lovingkindness* and truth; who keeps lovingkindness for thousands, who forgives iniquity, transgression and sin; yet He will by no means leave the guilty unpunished.

This self-revelation of Yahweh synchronizes with who we know Yeshua to be. First, Yahweh says here that He is "compassionate and gracious…abounding in lovingkindness." Doesn't this line up with what we know about Jesus? Isn't Messiah also "compassionate and gracious…abounding in lovingkindness"? Notice also that Yahweh says that He "forgives iniquity, transgression and sin; yet He will by no means leave the guilty unpunished." Didn't Yeshua say the same thing? Jesus came to "[forgive] iniquity, transgression and sin." Yet as the Book of Revelation reveals, He will not let the guilty go unpunished. Yahweh, the God we read about in the Hebrew Bible, or Old Testament, and His Son, Jesus, who is revealed to us in the New Testament, are one. Jesus said, "He who has seen Me has seen the Father" (John 14:9) and, "I and the Father are one" (John 10:30).

The Hebrew word translated as "one" in Deuteronomy 6:4—"The LORD is one"—is *echad*. This same Hebrew word is used in Genesis 2:24, which says a man shall "be joined to his wife; and they shall become one [*echad*] flesh." Notice here that this word *echad* is used to describe a compound unity rather than a singular unity. The man and woman are *joined to become one*.

I bring this up to point out that traditional Jews reject Messiah Jesus because, they say, "If God had a son who is to be worshipped, there would be two gods, and we believe in one God." Yet the Hebrew word in Deuteronomy 6:4, *echad* (again, translated as "one"), does not necessitate that God is a singular unity. The great I Am is one, but He is multidimensional. Although God has revealed Himself as Father, Son, and Holy Spirit, He is one. He is not three Gods, but one God—the great I Am is multidimensional. Even as we cannot comprehend that He is self-existent and came from nowhere but has always been, so we cannot fathom that the Father, Son, and Spirit are one and the same God.

This commandment calls us to recognize and affirm the oneness of God, a truth that pervades both the Hebrew Bible and the New Testament. By honoring the precept of the oneness of the eternal Lord (Deut. 6:4), we affirm the continuity between the Torah and the New Testament.

THE COMMAND TO LOVE THE ETERNAL LORD

You shall love the LORD your God with all your heart
and with all your soul and with all your might.
—DEUTERONOMY 6:5

THIS LAW IS part of Judaism's most important prayer declaration, called the Shema. It is recited by Orthodox Jews every morning and evening and are the last words a Jew is to utter before death.

When Rabbi Yeshua was asked what the most important commandment was, He answered by quoting this mitzvah from Deuteronomy 6:5. This helps us gain a sense of how Jewish the New Testament is.

> "Teacher, which is the great commandment in the Law?" And He said to him, "'You shall love the Lord your God with all your heart, and with all your soul, and with all your mind.'"
> —MATTHEW 22:36–37

Sometimes we think of God as so big and far away that it escapes us that He can be moved by our love for Him. Yet this commandment and central precept of the Torah—to love the Lord our God with all our heart, soul, and might—shows us how important it is to God to be loved by His people.

Notice this law commands us to love God with *all* our *heart*, *soul*, and *might*, representing our entirety. But how do we love

God? Consider that loving God in Judaism is not first an experience, feeling, or even a belief, but is rather an action. Jews believe that souls should be evaluated not so much by their intellectual beliefs but by their concrete actions. For Jews, one loves God by studying the Torah, keeping the mitzvot, practicing *tikkun olam* (Hebrew for "repairing the world"), and doing good unto others.

We can see this mindset of expressing our love and faith through action in the New Testament. Consider both the words of Rabbi Yeshua and those of the apostle James, Jesus' half-brother.

> He who has My commandments and keeps them is the one who loves Me.
>
> —JOHN 14:21

> What use is it, my brethren, if someone says he has faith but he has no works? Can that faith save him? If a brother or sister is without clothing and in need of daily food, and one of you says to them, "Go in peace, be warmed and be filled," and yet you do not give them what is necessary for their body, what use is that? Even so faith, if it has no works, is dead, being by itself. But someone may well say, "You have faith and I have works; show me your faith without the works, and I will show you my faith by my works." You believe that God is one. You do well; the demons also believe, and shudder. But are you willing to recognize, you foolish fellow, that faith without works is useless?
>
> —JAMES 2:14–20

Loving God, then, is not first an emotion but is a disposition that determines our behavior and attitude. Loving God is our orientation and posture. We are commanded to love God because He is deserving of our honor and adoration, and because love is the essence of life. God is love (1 John 4:8).

It needs to be stated, however, that the ability to love God is itself a grace we receive from Him. As 1 John 4:19 says, "We love, because He first loved us." This understanding calls us to realize that our capacity to love God begins with His initiative to reveal Himself to us.

Because loving God requires action, it involves bringing our thoughts and words into obedience to His lordship. As 2 Corinthians 10:5 states, "We are destroying speculations and every lofty thing raised up against the knowledge of God, and we are taking every thought captive to the obedience of Christ." This means we show our love for God by aligning our minds with His will.

Honoring the mitzvah to love the eternal God (Deut. 6:5) is not an abstract concept but a daily, lived reality. Loving God involves obeying His commandments, dedicating our thoughts to Him, and following Yeshua. By striving to love God with all our heart, soul, and might, we fulfill this central and foundational commandment and are brought into the experience of His fullness.

THE PRECEPT OF TORAH STUDY

These words, which I am commanding you today, shall be on your heart. You shall teach them diligently to your sons and shall talk of them when you sit in your house and when you walk by the way and when you lie down and when you rise up. You shall bind them as a sign on your hand and they shall be as frontals on your forehead. You shall write them on the doorposts of your house and on your gates.
—Deuteronomy 6:6–9

Studying and immersing ourselves in the Torah is considered the highest form of worship in Rabbinic Judaism, and it is the chief responsibility of parents to teach the Torah to their children.

In modern Judaism this focus extends beyond the written Torah to include the Oral Law, known as the Mishnah, and its commentary, the Gemara. Together these form the Talmud. Rabbinic Judaism holds that God gave Moses not only the written books of Genesis through Deuteronomy on Mount Sinai but also oral instructions on how to carry out the commandments contained therein. These oral laws or instructions, revered in modern Orthodox Judaism, were eventually documented between the second and third centuries BC and were referred to as "the tradition of the elders" during Yeshua's time. We see this clearly demonstrated in Mark 7:5 when the Pharisees and scribes asked Yeshua, "Why do Your disciples not walk according to the *tradition of the elders*?" (emphasis added).

Rabbi Yeshua's position on the Oral Law caused a critical division between Himself and the Jewish religious leaders. He viewed much of it as the traditions of men rather than divine commandments. In Mark 7, Yeshua challenged the Pharisees and scribes for placing these traditions above God's commandments. Quoting Isaiah, He said, "This people honors Me with their lips, but their heart is far away from Me. But in vain do they worship Me, *teaching as doctrines the precepts of men*" (vv. 6–7, emphasis added). Yeshua highlighted how their adherence to tradition often invalidated the Word of God.

Despite this critique, we can appreciate Judaism's devotion to studying God's Word even if we do not accept all aspects of rabbinism (the teachings and practices of the rabbis). This devotion contrasts sharply with the lack of scriptural engagement among many who claim to be Yeshua's disciples. In some circles there is a greater emphasis on singing the most popular worship songs than on studying the Scriptures. Many "believers" love the "worship concerts" at the beginning of church services on Sunday mornings but do not study the Bible. While worship is essential, it cannot replace the need for a deep, disciplined study of God's Word.

Without a thorough knowledge of the Scriptures, we won't know how to walk with HaShem. The Scriptures are God's self-revelation to us, showing us who He is and how to walk with Him.

David said to the Lord in Psalm 119: "I will meditate on Your precepts....Your word is a lamp to my feet and a light to my path" (vv. 15, 105). Without God's Word hidden in our hearts, we cannot navigate through life or the spiritual challenges we face. Unfortunately, too many believers have not made studying, memorizing, and internalizing God's Word a priority.

As a matter of godly practice and habit, I encourage reading at least one chapter from the Old Testament and one chapter from the New Testament each day. This practice should not be dependent on emotional inspiration but should be a daily discipline, much like athletes who train consistently regardless of how they feel. Paul challenges us to discipline ourselves for the purpose of godliness (1 Tim. 4:7). Some days you may feel inspired and focused while reading Scripture; other days you may struggle to see its relevance. Regardless, stick with the discipline. God sees your efforts, and He is a rewarder of those who diligently seek Him (Heb. 11:6).

The precept of Torah study (Deut. 6:6–9) calls us to a devoted engagement with God's Word. By committing to daily study, we honor God, deepen our understanding of His will, equip ourselves to navigate life's challenges, and train ourselves in righteousness.

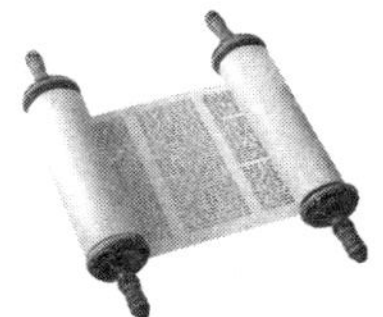

THE PRECEPT OF THE MEZUZAH

You shall write them on the doorposts of
your house and on your gates.
—Deuteronomy 6:9

The mezuzah is a small scroll of parchment on which are written two biblical passages: Deuteronomy 6:4–9 and Deuteronomy 11:13–21. This scroll is then placed in a box that is affixed to the doorpost of Jewish homes. This practice of posting the mezuzah on the entryways of our homes and offices serves to sanctify our living and working spaces with God's blessing and presence. The mezuzah not only consecrates our homes and offices but also reminds those who affix them of God's watchful eye over their lives, helping us stay devoted to Him.

In Judaism, the mezuzah symbolizes a commitment to the Lord and His commandments. As we pass by and touch the mezuzah, we take comfort in knowing that we are loved by our Creator and that He is watching over us. This daily ritual reinforces our dedication to living according to God's Word and keeps His presence at the forefront of our consciousness.

Prophetically, the principle behind the mezuzah can be practically applied to our lives by placing in our homes and workplaces physical reminders of God's presence. Early followers of Yeshua used symbols like the fish (ichthys) to remind themselves of and identify with Yeshua. Today many followers of The Way hang crosses or display sacred artwork in their homes. These physical memorials serve a similar purpose as the mezuzah, keeping God's presence central in our lives. Although Acts 17:24 reminds us that God no longer dwells in temples made with hands, we can still glorify His name and sanctify the physical environments we live and work in.

We can easily be influenced by our environment and the forces that surround us. By filling our homes with objects that reflect our faith, we cultivate an awareness of God. This can include framed Scripture verses or biblical artwork. For instance, I have pictures of Jerusalem and the Western Wall, a shofar, a menorah (the seven-branched candle that was in the Temple and is the symbol of Judaism today), and other biblically themed items in my home. These pieces serve as constant reminders of my faith and the nearness of the Most High.

Honoring the precept of the mezuzah (Deut. 6:9) creates an environment that honors God and helps us remember He is with us. This deep-rooted Jewish tradition can be embraced by all believers.

TO KILL OFF THE SEVEN NATIONS AND SHOW NO MERCY TO IDOL WORSHIPPERS

When the LORD your God brings you into the land where you are entering to possess it, and clears away many nations before you, the Hittites and the Girgashites and the Amorites and the Canaanites and the Perizzites and the Hivites and the Jebusites, seven nations greater and stronger than you, and when the LORD your God delivers them before you and you defeat them, then you shall utterly destroy them. You shall make no covenant with them and show no favor to them.

—DEUTERONOMY 7:1–2

THE LORD COMMANDED Israel to utterly destroy the idolatrous nations occupying the Promised Land. This directive, reiterated in Deuteronomy 20:17, where God commands Israel to "utterly destroy" these nations, may sound harsh to modern ears. However, Yahweh knew that if His people did not annihilate these nations, they would end up following them into idolatry and defilement. The divine command was meant to protect Israel from corrupting influences.

The seven nations were all descendants of Canaan, son of Ham and grandson of Noah. These seven nations were hardcore idol worshippers. Today we may not comprehend how worshipping a statue of a false deity could be so evil that the person would need to be annihilated. But consider that "part of their cult worship was to sacrifice children to the gods....[Modern] archaeologists also have found mounds of children's bones by their altars. These nations were also involved in various sexual immoralities like incest, bestiality and temple orgies."[22] (See Leviticus 18:27 and Deuteronomy 12:31.) In fact, these nations were so perverse that Rabbi Akiva, a second-century Jewish scholar, "reported that he saw a son bind up his father and feed him to ravaging dogs in service of one [of] his idols."[23]

It's hard for many of us who have grown up in relatively peaceful and safe environments to understand this concept: If you don't destroy evil, it will destroy you. Israel was surrounded by cruel, savage, violent neighbors, and if they didn't destroy these sinful nations around them, they would be destroyed.

In reading this law in which the Lord commanded Israel to kill off the seven nations they encountered, many will think God is cruel and inhumane. The Lord was not being merciless; rather, Yahweh was delivering His people out of a barbaric society, giving them His Law so that they would become a just and compassionate people in the earth.

Sometimes the only way to deal with evil is to ruthlessly cut it out. Consider that during World War II, had the United States not dropped the atomic bomb that effectively ended the war, *we* may have been destroyed and consumed by Nazi Germany.

The Torah expresses spiritual realities in physical terms. Our enemy is not a nation but sin, and sin must be obliterated. Consider how Yeshua's words mirror Deuteronomy 7:1–2 (the law commanding Israel to destroy the idolatrous nations they encountered) in relation to how a believer is to deal with sin:

> If your hand or your foot causes you to stumble, cut it off and throw it from you; it is better for you to enter life crippled or lame, than to have two hands or two feet and be cast into the eternal fire. If your eye causes you to stumble, pluck it out and throw it from you. It is better for you to enter life with one eye,

> than to have two eyes and be cast into the fiery hell.
>
> —Matthew 18:8–9

This metaphorical language makes plain that we must deal decisively with sin. Just as Israel was commanded to eradicate the seven nations to prevent corruption, believers are called to eliminate anything in our lives that leads us into defilement. If a particular behavior or habit leads us to sin, we must take radical steps to remove it from our lives. For example, if having a glass of wine leads to alcohol misuse, one should abstain from alcohol altogether. If watching certain TV programs causes lust, turn off the TV or change the channel. If a relationship tempts us to sin, break that relationship off. Don't put yourself in situations where you are tempted to compromise. Drive evil out of your life.

The principle of eradicating sources of temptation also appears in Numbers 33:55, where the Lord warns Israel, "But if you do not drive out the inhabitants of the land from before you, then it shall come about that those whom you let remain of them will become as pricks in your eyes and as thorns in your sides." Tolerating sin leads to our own harm.

Having pastored for twenty-five years, there were times when I needed to remove troublemakers from within our congregation. Some thought this was harsh and that I "lacked love," but I knew if I allowed them to stay, the evil and rebellion in them would have spread into the whole congregation. If I had tolerated them, my ministry would have been compromised and I would have ended up the one who got removed.

Again, evil must be dealt with, and we should not put ourselves in situations where we are tempted to compromise; instead, we must actively drive evil influences from our lives. When I first became a believer in 1978, I had a large collection of records from bands like Led Zeppelin, Mott the Hoople, Black Sabbath, and many others. Although I enjoyed the music, I realized it was not conducive to my new life in Messiah, so I took all the records and threw them into a big, commercial trash bin because I didn't want anything to defile my relationship with God. This act of "violent" elimination protected my newfound faith.

The precepts to kill off the seven nations and show no mercy to idol worshippers (Deut. 7:1–2) remind us to be radical in our approach to sin and ruthless in our devotion to God!

TO FORM NO MARITAL BONDS WITH IDOL WORSHIPPERS

You shall not intermarry with them; you shall not give your daughters to their sons, nor shall you take their daughters for your sons.
—Deuteronomy 7:3

Much like the command to kill off the seven nations and show no mercy to idol worshippers, this law prohibited Israel from intermarrying with the pagan nations surrounding them. The account of King Solomon shows the consequences of disobedience to this command. Despite his wisdom, Solomon loved many foreign women from nations with whom the Lord had warned the Israelites not to associate. These women led Solomon's heart astray, turning him to other gods. As he aged, Solomon was not wholly devoted to the Most High as his father, David, had been. He went after Ashtoreth, the goddess of the Sidonians, and Milcom, the detestable idol of the Ammonites, doing evil in the sight of the Lord. God was angry with Solomon as a result and declared that the kingdom would be torn from him and given to his servant. (See 1 Kings 11:1–6, 9, 11.)

Even today, within Orthodox Judaism, marrying a non-Jew is deeply frowned upon, and in some situations the offender is effectively cut off from the Orthodox community. Although rates of intermarriage (Jews marrying non-Jews) have sharply risen in recent decades, Orthodox Rabbis will not officiate an interfaith wedding. The reason for this goes back to this commandment in

Deuteronomy 7:3, which was given to protect Israel from assimilation and idol-worship, and to ensure their exclusive devotion to the God of Israel.

The principle of not forming intimate relationships with those who are not in a covenant relationship with the God of Israel, who is the God and Father of Yeshua the Messiah, is reiterated in the New Testament. Over my forty-five years of walking with the Lord, I have often seen professing believers enter relationships with unbelievers, leading them to spiritually backslide and even abandon their relationship with Yeshua completely. This phenomenon is especially noticeable among older single women who, out of loneliness, compromise their faith.

Paul addressed this directly in 2 Corinthians 6:14–18:

> Do not be bound together with unbelievers; for what partnership have righteousness and lawlessness, or what fellowship has light with darkness? Or what harmony has Christ with Belial, or what has a believer in common with an unbeliever? Or what agreement has the temple of God with idols? For we are the temple of the living God; just as God said, "I will dwell in them and walk among them; and I will be their God, and they shall be My people. Therefore, come out from their midst and be separate," says the Lord. "And do not touch what is unclean...," says the Lord Almighty.

Just as ancient Israel was commanded to form no marital bonds with idol worshippers (Deut. 7:3) to preserve their faith, so too are believers today called to separate ourselves from relationships that could compromise our spiritual integrity. If you are single, it is crucial to decide not to enter an intimate relationship with an unbeliever.

TO TAKE NO OBJECT FROM IDOLATRY INTO OUR POSSESSION

> The *graven images* of their gods you are to burn with fire; you shall not covet the silver or the gold that is on them, nor take it for yourselves, or you will be snared by it, for it is an abomination to the LORD your God. You shall not bring an abomination into your house, and like it come under the ban; you shall utterly detest it and you shall utterly abhor it, for it is something banned.
> —DEUTERONOMY 7:25–26, EMPHASIS ADDED

THIS LAW COMMANDS the Israelites not only to utterly destroy the graven images of foreign gods but also to not covet or take the silver or gold that was on them. These items were considered abominations to the one true holy and pure God, and bringing them into one's home would cause the inhabitants to be ensnared by their evil influence.

This mitzvah is still very relevant today. By definition an image is a representation or visual impression of something. When a person takes something that is an expression of evil into their hands, they have conceptually violated this commandment. This includes taking objects, artwork, or sculptures from pagan cultures into our homes. Many naively do this when they vacation in non-Judeo-Christian cultures and bring home an idolatrous image, such as a mini statue representing a Hindu god from India.

Many believers think dressing up as devils, witches, ghosts, and demons on Halloween is just innocent fun. Not only is it dangerous because it opens us and our children to evil, but it is abhorrent to God, just as this commandment clearly states. Participating in such activities, even if they seem harmless, can have serious spiritual consequences.

Similarly, many of God's people watch horror movies and feel it is just entertainment. Others read books or play video games that are horror- or fear-based. But when we choose to engage with content that has the powers of darkness behind it, we open ourselves to the work of evil in our lives. This can lead to spiritual oppression and a desensitization to the very real dangers of the occult.

May the precept to take no object from idolatry into our possession (Deut. 7:25–26) encourage you to guard your house and life against the power of evil in any form.

THE PRECEPT OF BLESSING THE ALMIGHTY FOR THE FOOD WE RECEIVE

When you have eaten and are satisfied, *you shall bless* the Lord your God for the good land which He has given you.
—Deuteronomy 8:10, emphasis added

In Judaism, a prayer is offered before and after eating. Biblically, grace—known in Hebrew as Birkat Hamazon—is said after the meal. The blessing before a meal is not commanded in the Torah but was added by the rabbis.

This command to bless and thank the Lord after eating helps us maintain a spirit of gratitude to God. Obeying this biblical precept is not rooted in our emotions but is about choosing to be thankful. We live in a culture of entitlement. Things have come so easy for some of us that we have become spoiled. We must resist the spirit of entitlement, and one of the best ways we can do this is to daily give praise to God for our food.

Some are tempted to think, "God didn't give me this food; I bought it" or "I grew it." But consider Deuteronomy 8:17–18: "You may say in your heart, 'My power and the strength of my hand made me this wealth.' But you shall remember the Lord your God, for it is He who is giving you power to make wealth, that He may confirm His covenant which He swore to your fathers, as it is this day." The Lord spoke this to Israel to warn them about the sin of presumption and protect them from developing an arrogant spirit.

When we take the blessings God gives us—including our spouses, children, employers, and friends—for granted, we set ourselves up for unhappiness. We cannot be personally happy or pleasing to God without being thankful. In a day when many people take most things for granted, giving thanks at each meal is a reality check that keeps us humble and helps us remember that we are blessed.

I like to watch a reality TV series in which ten people are dropped off in the wilderness and must survive using only their bushcraft, hunting, and fishing skills. Often they must go without eating because they weren't able to catch fish or trap any game. After being hungry for a few days and then finally catching a fish, they become almost ecstatic, falling to their knees and sometimes crying. Even those contestants who had not previously mentioned God look up and say, "Thank You, God."

But, beloved, it shouldn't take deprivation to make us thankful. Instead of appreciating the gift of health after we get sick, wouldn't it be much better to be thankful for it in advance and possibly avoid the trial altogether?

Notice also that the command to bless the Lord after eating speaks of satisfaction: "When you have eaten *and are satisfied*, you shall bless the LORD your God" (Deut. 8:10, emphasis added). Reflect on this a moment: God wants us to be satisfied. He wants us to be happy. And as we saw earlier, a happy person is not someone who has everything they want but rather someone who is thankful for what they have. Let's bless the Lord for all the good things we have in our lives and not take anything for granted.

TO BE IN REVERENT AWE OF THE ETERNAL LORD

You shall fear the LORD your God; you shall serve Him and cling to Him, and you shall swear by His name.
—DEUTERONOMY 10:20

THE COMMANDMENT TO fear the Lord is central and fundamental to walking in harmony with God. It is a positive commandment, not a prohibition, as it says, "You *shall* fear the LORD your God."

Psalm 25:14 reminds us that "the secret of the LORD is for those who fear Him, and He will make them know His covenant." Many have believed that the fear of God is opposite the love of God. These two are not opposites but different facets of the same diamond. Consider what Isaiah said in describing the coming Messiah:

> Then a shoot will spring from the stem of Jesse, and a branch from his roots will bear fruit. The Spirit of the LORD will rest on Him, the spirit of wisdom and understanding, the spirit of counsel and strength, the spirit of knowledge and the fear of the LORD. *And He will delight in the fear of the Lord.*
> —ISAIAH 11:1–3, EMPHASIS ADDED

The Scriptures are saturated with the teaching of the fear of God. Proverbs 9:10 says, "The fear of the LORD is the beginning of wisdom, and the knowledge of the Holy One is understanding."

The fear of God's judgment serves as a powerful motivator for obedience. King David feared God's judgment if he were to sin, and this kept him walking in God's ways. He wrote, "My flesh trembles for fear of You, and I am afraid of Your judgments" (Ps. 119:120).

Much modern teaching reduces the fear of God to simply honoring Him, revering Him, and being in awe of Him. All of these are good and right, but because many pastors and preachers have been conformed to the spirit of the world, they fail to preach the good old-fashioned fear of the Lord that keeps us from sinning.

Consider what the Bible says about Job: "That man was blameless, upright, fearing God and turning away from evil" (Job 1:1). The pure fear of the Most High keeps us and protects us from sin. When I don't feel emotionally connected to God, I continue to obey Him because I fear Him. It is not a fear that paralyzes me but a fear that recognizes that if I walk in disobedience, His discipline will fall upon me. By the grace of God, the fear of His judgment keeps me committed even when I don't feel "in love" with Him.

We can't control our emotions. Some days we sense God's presence and feel His love. Other days, seemingly for no reason at all, we just wake up in the morning and feel disconnected. The fear of the Lord keeps us moving forward in obedience in times when we feel nothing.

Conversely, Paul describes the unredeemed with these words: "There is no fear of God before their eyes" (Rom. 3:18). That is why they engage in grievous sins against their Creator. As the Psalms reveal, "Transgression speaks to the ungodly within his heart; *there is no fear of God before his eyes*" (Ps. 36:1, emphasis added).

The fear of the Lord is actually a beautiful gift that Yahweh places in the hearts of His elect. Moses told Israel that the Lord God revealed Himself to them *in power* at Mount Sinai *to put His fear in their souls* in order to prevent them from sinning:

> All the people perceived the thunder and the lightning flashes and the sound of the trumpet and the mountain smoking; and when the people saw it, they trembled and stood at a distance. Then they said to Moses, "Speak to us yourself and we will listen; but let not God speak to us, or we will die." Moses said to the people, "Do not be afraid; for God has come in order to test you, and *in order that the fear of Him may remain with you, so that you may not sin.*"
>
> —Exodus 20:18–20, emphasis added

Some think that now that we are under the new covenant, we are no longer to fear God in this way because God has "delivered us from fear." (See, for example, 1 John 4:18.) But the fears God has delivered us from are the ones HaSatan (Hebrew for "the adversary") brings against humanity, not the fear of God. In fact, when we fear God, we are delivered from all the enemy's fears. Isaiah 8:12–13 says, "You are not to say, 'It is a conspiracy!' in regard to all that this people call a conspiracy, and you are not to fear what they fear or be in dread of it. It is the Lord of hosts whom you should regard as holy. And He shall be your fear, and He shall be your dread."

Messiah Jesus taught the pure fear of the Lord in Matthew 10:28 when He said, "Do not fear those who kill the body but are unable to kill the soul; but rather fear Him who is able to destroy both soul and body in hell." Fearing God alone delivers us from every other fear!

Consider Jeremiah's words in prophesying about the new covenant: "I will give them one heart and one way, that they may fear Me always, for their own good and for the good of their children after them. I will make an everlasting covenant with them that I will not turn away from them, to do them good; and *I will put the fear of Me in their hearts so that they will not turn away from Me. I will rejoice over them to do them good*" (Jer. 32:39–41, emphasis added).

Yes, the fear of the Lord is good, and we should desire it, like

David, who said, "Teach me Your way, O LORD; I will walk in Your truth; *unite my heart to fear Your name*" (Ps. 86:11, emphasis added).

Finally, consider the words of Solomon, the wisest man on the earth: "The fear of the LORD is a fountain of life, that one may avoid the snares of death" (Prov. 14:27). Let's embrace the precept to be in reverent awe of the eternal Lord (Deut. 10:20)!

THE PRECEPT OF PRAYER

Thou shalt fear the Lord thy God; him shalt thou serve, and *to him shalt thou cleave*, and swear by his name.
—Deuteronomy 10:20, kjv, emphasis added

This mitzvah commands us to "cleave" to God. The Hebrew word is *devekut*, which conveys a sense of attachment, being glued or joined together, holding fast, and becoming one. In Judaism, fastening oneself to God is brought about by continually keeping Him in our hearts and minds. This is accomplished through prayer and faithfully walking in His ways.

Second Chronicles 27:6 says, "So Jotham became mighty because he ordered his ways before the Lord his God." To be joined together with God, we must "walk in His ways." How can we have fellowship with Him if our lives are out of sync and going a different direction from Him? Yeshua said oneness with Abba Father is progressively achieved by clinging to Him: "He who has My commandments and keeps them is the one who loves Me; and he who loves Me will be loved by My Father, and I will love him and will disclose Myself to him....If anyone loves Me, he will keep My word; and My Father will love him, and We will come to him and make Our abode with him" (John 14:21, 23).

According to Jewish tradition, associating with great Torah scholars also enhances our ability to cling to God. By being in close relationship with those who deeply understand and teach

God's Word, we grow in spiritual strength and sanctification. The Judaic principle of honoring those who teach the Torah extends into the New Testament, where Paul instructs believers to give "double honor" to church elders who labor in preaching and teaching (1 Tim. 5:17).

Honoring the precept of prayer by "cleaving" to God (Deut. 10:20) is characterized by communicating with the Holy Spirit from our inner soul and seeking His favor. Wherever we go, wherever we are, He is as close as our prayer: "Where can I go from Your Spirit? Or where can I flee from Your presence? If I ascend to heaven, You are there; if I make my bed in Sheol, behold, You are there" (Ps. 139:7–8).

TO NOT ADD TO OR DIMINISH THE PRECEPTS OF THE TORAH

Whatever I command you, you shall be careful to do; you shall not add to nor take away from it.
—Deuteronomy 12:32

The commandment to neither add to nor take away from the precepts of the Torah is critical to preserve the purity and integrity of God's Word. Notice that in this scripture, God is speaking to His people in the first person. Similarly, the Lord speaks in the first person in Deuteronomy 4:2 when repeating this commandment: "You shall not add to the word which *I am commanding you*, nor take away from it, that you may keep the commandments of the Lord your God which I command you" (emphasis added). This warns us of the severe danger of taking the liberty to alter His words.

Through the centuries, however, the rabbis added numerous laws to the written Torah, creating a heavy burden for the people. By the time Rabbi Yeshua came along, this had become a significant issue. We see this in the Gospel of Mark when the Pharisees and scribes questioned Him, saying, "Why do Your disciples not walk according to the tradition of the elders, but eat their bread with impure hands?" Messiah responded by accusing them of setting aside God's commandments in favor of their traditions (Mark 7:5, 9).

This issue is not confined to when Jesus walked the earth.

Even today many church leaders add to or diminish God's Word. Some ignore or downplay parts of Scripture they find uncomfortable, such as repentance, sin, and hell, while others emphasize nonbiblical doctrines such as purgatory, infant baptism, or name-it-and-claim-it prosperity gospels. Others alter God's Word by using it to come up with fantastical prophetic interpretations that are a misrepresentation of the Scriptures' truth in order to gain social media views.

In keeping with the Torah, the apostle Paul warned against this, saying, "But even if we, or an angel from heaven, should preach to you a gospel contrary to what we have preached to you, he is to be accursed! As we have said before, so I say again now, if any man is preaching to you a gospel contrary to what you received, he is to be accursed!" (Gal. 1:8–9).

The Book of Revelation also sternly warns against altering God's Word: "I testify to everyone who hears the words of the prophecy of this book: if anyone adds to them, God will add to him the plagues which are written in this book; and if anyone takes away from the words of the book of this prophecy, God will take away his part from the tree of life and from the holy city, which are written in this book" (Rev. 22:18–19).

The commandment not to add to or diminish the words of the Torah (Deut. 12:32) warns us to be diligent in upholding the integrity of the Scriptures without alteration. This means faithfully teaching and living out the entirety of God's Word, acknowledging the full scope of its instruction without adding anything to or subtracting from it.

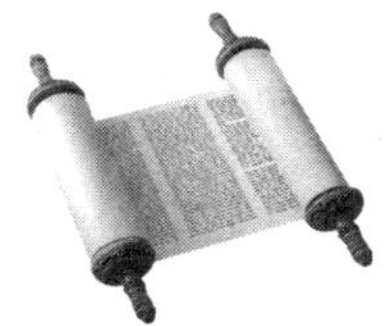

TO NOT CUT ONESELF OR PULL ONE'S HAIR OUT FOR THE DEAD

> You are the sons of the Lord your God; you shall not cut yourselves nor shave your forehead for the sake of the dead. For you are a holy people to the Lord your God, and the Lord has chosen you to be a people for His own possession out of all the peoples who are on the face of the earth.
>
> —Deuteronomy 14:1–2

This commandment prohibits excessive mourning practices, such as self-mutilation or hair-pulling, when a loved one passes away. While mourning is a significant and necessary part of the grieving process, this law teaches that it should not lead to self-destructive behaviors or become an obstacle to moving forward.

Mourning holds a vital place in Judaism and involves several phases to ensure proper emotional and spiritual healing. A seven-day period known as shiva (Hebrew for *seven*) follows the burial and is a formal time of mourning by the immediate family. During this time, the family gathers to honor and celebrate the life of the deceased, creating a support system for healing. Following shiva, a thirty-day mourning period begins, during which mourners gradually return to normal life but abstain from celebrations like weddings and parties. If the deceased was a parent, children extend this abstention for a full year, reflecting a deeper level of respect and remembrance.

This structured approach stresses the importance of honoring the deceased while also acknowledging the need to move forward. Mourning should not lead to a state of paralysis or continuous despair. Instead, it should serve as a time of reflection, healing, and eventual return to life's activities. After an appropriate season of mourning, one must look up, praise Adonai, and walk in the joy of the Lord.

I have seen cases in which a loved one passes and the immediate relative takes no time at all to mourn. Some have even returned to work the day after the funeral. When my dad passed away, the Lord brought me to a deep place in His Spirit where I took time and drank from the well of eternity. I am thankful that I was able to have this time of processing and healing in Him so I could move forward on solid footing. It is important to take time to mourn, and we must remember and practice this in our fast-paced culture today.

On the other hand, I have seen people who would not let go of the mourning period and continued living in a state of deep depression and despair, "clinging" to the loved one who had passed. As hard as it is to say, this is unhealthy and ultimately dishonors God, who is light and life.

From this precept not to cut oneself or pull one's hair out for the dead (Deut. 14:1–2) we learn that we must properly mourn lost loved ones but then move forward with God.

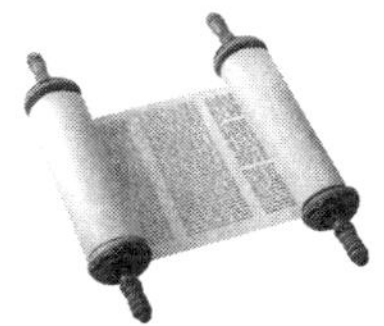

TO NOT REFRAIN FROM HELPING THE POOR AND GIVING

If there is a poor man with you, one of your brothers, in any of your towns in your land which the LORD your God is giving you, you shall not harden your heart, nor close your hand from your poor brother; but you shall freely open your hand to him, and shall generously lend him sufficient for his need in whatever he lacks.
—DEUTERONOMY 15:7–8

THE ORIGINAL INTENT of this and similar laws was to create a compassionate society where every member is cared for. The Torah instructs that fellow Israelites who become poor should be sustained. This entailed not only providing for their immediate needs but also integrating them into the community by offering them the dignity of work. The poor man would become a "hired man," working for his brother who took him in, thus preserving his sense of purpose and self-respect.

Charity has always been at the heart of Judaism. Studies have shown that the US Jewish community gives the most of any religious group. They even give more money to non-Jewish organizations than other religious groups give to those outside their faith.[24] *Tzedakah* is the Hebrew word for *philanthropy* and *charity*. Many Jewish homes have a tzedakah box to collect coins that will be used to help others. This practice, like other forms of charity in Judaism, is related to social justice in its most positive, God-honoring form. We should give when we see someone in need. The one who gives today may be the one who is on the receiving end tomorrow.

The famous Torah scholar Maimonides, who codified Jewish law, addressed not only the need to give but also the spirit one must have in doing so. He wrote: "Whoever gives tzedakah to the poor with a sour expression…loses his merit. One should instead give cheerfully and joyfully, and emphasize with him in his sorrow."[25]

Everyone benefits when charity is given. The poor benefit by having their needs met, and the donor receives the gift of sharing in the work of the Almighty. Both the person who gives and the one who receives are playing a part in modeling God's ways. The point is to think of ourselves as part of the brotherhood of humanity and to be sensitive and respond to those in need.

On the other hand, we are not called to support those who lack because they refuse to work. Rather, we are to come alongside those who fall into need due to circumstances beyond their control. We recognize that a man is to do all he can to provide for himself rather than relying on other people's charity. Paul wrote, "If anyone is not willing to work, then he is not to eat" (2 Thess. 3:10).

In Israel, there are many who inappropriately depend on the charity of other Jews. Because it is so stressed in Judaism that Jews are to take care of one another, there is, unfortunately, a demographic in Israel whose full-time occupation is begging. Yet, again, the Bible is clear that we have a responsibility not only to give but to do all we can to make a living for ourselves, not relying on others' charity.

Giving is at the soul of Judaism, as it should be among Yeshua's followers. Paul's exhortation in Galatians 6:10 to "do good to all people, and especially to those who are of the household of the faith" echoes the principle underlying this commandment. In Acts, the early believers shared their possessions openhandedly so no one among them was in need (Acts 2:44–45). We are to extend kindness and care to all individuals, with an intensified focus on helping fellow believers.

Rabbi Yeshua said, "Truly I tell you, whatever you did for one of the least of these brothers and sisters of mine, you did for me" (Matt. 25:40, NIV). This reinforces the idea that caring for the needy is not just a social obligation but a spiritual act. Throughout the Scriptures we are repeatedly called to show compassion to the poor. Proverbs 19:17 states, "Whoever is kind to the poor lends to the LORD, and he will reward them for what they have done" (NIV). Similarly, James, the Jewish apostle, emphasized the importance of offering tangible assistance: "If a brother or sister is without clothing and in need of daily food, and one of you says to them, 'Go in peace, be warmed and be filled,' and yet you do not give them what is necessary for their body, what use is that?" (Jas. 2:15–16).

This need for faith and love to be manifest by action is thoroughly highlighted throughout the entire New Testament. First John 3:17–18 says, "But if anyone has the world's goods and sees his brother in need, yet closes his heart against him, how does God's love abide in him? Little children, let us not love in word or talk but in deed and in truth" (ESV).

Today many congregations seek to carry out the principle of this law through community aid programs and charitable initiatives such as food pantries. But there are countless ways to model the essence of this mitzvah. I remember sitting in my backyard over twenty years ago and praying that I could start a company to provide jobs for the many good people at the congregation I led who had no work. The Lord answered that prayer beyond anything I imagined at the time—Discovering the Jewish Jesus now employs over forty people who are doing an amazing job in playing their part to spread the gospel around the whole world!

The commandment to help the needy (Deut. 15:7–8) conveys the heart of Rabbi Yeshua. May this precept motivate us to take real, actionable steps to help those around us in need.

TO BE HAPPY ON THE PILGRIMAGE FESTIVALS

And you shall rejoice in your feast, you and your son and your daughter and your male and female servants and the Levite and the stranger and the orphan and the widow who are in your towns.
—Deuteronomy 16:14

There are three pilgrim feasts: Passover (Pesach), Pentecost (Shavuot), and the Feast of Tabernacles (Sukkot). Why three? The number three holds a special place both in Judaism and in God's written Word.

First, *time* is distinctly divided into three parts: past, present, and future. Consider that even God's sacred name, Yahweh, implies that He exists in the past, present, and future.

In Exodus 3:13–15, Moses asked God about His name:

> Then Moses said to God, "Behold, I am going to the sons of Israel, and I will say to them, 'The God of your fathers has sent me to you.' Now they may say to me, 'What is His name?' What shall I say to them?" God said to Moses, "I AM WHO I AM"; and He said, "Thus you shall say to the sons of Israel, 'I AM has sent me to you.'" God, furthermore, said to Moses, "Thus you shall say to the sons of Israel, 'The Lord [Yahweh], the God of your fathers, the God of Abraham, the God of Isaac, and the God of Jacob, has sent me to you.' This is My name forever, and this is My memorial-name to all generations."

In revealing Himself as "I Am Who I Am," the Lord discloses to us that He fills all three dimensions of time.

Secondly, consider that there were three divisions in the Tabernacle and Temple, the place where God met His people (Exod. 25:8)—the Outer Court, the Holy Place (or Inner Court), and the Holy of Holies. There are also three patriarchs of the Jewish faith—Abraham, Isaac, and Jacob. And in the New Testament the Lord manifested Himself three-dimensionally as Father, Son, and Spirit (Matt. 28:19), and Yeshua rose from the dead on the third day.

The number three represents divine wholeness, completeness, and perfection. Practicing this law of being happy on the three Pilgrim festivals trains us to have a disposition of joy year-round. By choosing to joyfully commemorate Passover, Pentecost (Shavuot), and the Feast of Tabernacles (Sukkot), we set a trajectory in our walks with God to live in joy as a lifestyle. Participating in these feasts allows us to hit the spiritual reset button.

The command to be happy in the Lord is a common thread in the Torah. The founder of Hasidic Judaism, Rabbi Nachman of Breslov (1772–1810), often said, "It is a great mitzvah to live in a state of happiness."[26] Why? Because in being happy we bond with God. Israel was judged for not rejoicing in Him: "Because you did not serve the Lord your God with joy and a glad heart, for the abundance of all things; therefore you shall serve your enemies whom the Lord will send against you…in the lack of all things" (Deut. 28:47–48). That is powerful. God commands and expects us to be happy because of His goodness and presence in our lives.

When you are feeling blue and ungrateful, remember the precept to be happy on the pilgrimage festivals (Deut. 16:14). It has been said that "most folks are about as happy as they make up their minds to be."[27] Our responsibility is to choose positivity by a conscious act of our will. Life can be hard, and this sometimes seems easier said than done. But at times we suffer more than we need to because our perspective is skewed. Instead of seeing what we have and rejoicing in the sufficiency of the Most High, we focus on our problems.

God is good, and when we view life from an eternal perspective, we can live in divine joy. As James instructs, "Consider it all joy, my brethren, when you encounter various trials, knowing that the testing of your faith produces endurance. And let endurance have its perfect result, so that you may be perfect and complete, lacking in nothing" (Jas. 1:2–4).

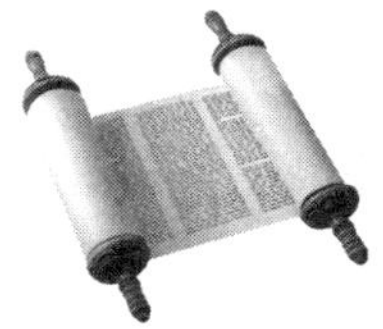

TO NOT GO UP TO JERUSALEM FOR A PILGRIMAGE FESTIVAL WITHOUT AN OFFERING

Three times in a year all your males shall appear before the LORD your God in the place which He chooses, at the Feast of Unleavened Bread and at the Feast of Weeks and at the Feast of Booths, and they shall *not appear before the LORD empty-handed*. Every man shall give as he is able, according to the blessing of the LORD your God which He has given you.
—DEUTERONOMY 16:16–17, EMPHASIS ADDED

WHEN THE PEOPLE of Israel traveled to Jerusalem for Pesach (Passover), Shavuot (Pentecost), and Sukkot (the Feast of Tabernacles), they were instructed not to appear before the Lord empty-handed. This underlines a broader principle: True worship involves not only our physical presence and acts of praise but also honoring God with our finances.

The Hebrew word for *offering* is *korban*, and it carries with it the idea of "drawing near." When we honor our Creator with our substance, we, in effect, draw near to Him. Through our tithes and offerings we rightly position our hearts and bring ourselves into proper alignment with our Creator. Without honoring the Most High with a sacrifice, our souls are out of alignment with the Blessed One. This is why David said in 1 Chronicles 21:24 that he would not offer to the Lord that which cost him nothing.

We see this spiritual principle illustrated from the very

beginning with Abraham. When Abraham, who is called the Father of all believers, Jew and Gentile alike (Rom. 4:9–12), met God's priest Melchizedek, Abraham offered up to the Lord through him a tenth of all he had (Gen. 14:18–20; Heb. 7:1–3).

May the command to not go up to Jerusalem for a pilgrimage festival without an offering (Deut. 16:16–17) remind us today that worship is not just about attending services, singing songs, or raising our hands in praise. True worshippers also honor God with their finances.

THE PRECEPTS OF APPOINTING JUDGES, OFFICERS, AND A KING

> You shall appoint for yourself judges and officers in all your towns which the LORD your God is giving you, according to your tribes, and they shall judge the people with righteous judgment....You shall surely set a king over you whom the LORD your God chooses, one from among your countrymen you shall set as king over yourselves; you may not put a foreigner over yourselves who is not your countryman.
>
> —DEUTERONOMY 16:18; 17:15

IN ANCIENT ISRAEL, the appointment of judges and officers ensured that justice was administered fairly and consistently. These leaders were responsible for maintaining societal order, addressing disputes, and upholding the law. Similarly, the establishment of a king provided centralized leadership and governance, ensuring that the nation remained unified under God's chosen leader.

The Torah gives direction about every facet of life. The Holy One, in His divine wisdom, knows that without government authority and structure, there is chaos.

Evil hates government because evil hates order. The nature of darkness is anarchy and confusion. The establishment of government and authority is crucial because evil thrives in chaos. God desires that His people live in the safety and security of a well-ordered and righteous society.

Due to humanity's fallen nature, people in governmental positions repeatedly have misused their power, causing many to rebel against civic and social structures. It is indeed unfortunate that so many political leaders have abused their authority, but in general, less-than-perfect government is better than no government at all.

In 2020 the United States witnessed a small movement crying to defund the police and reallocate resources to non-policing ways of addressing crime. Of course, all types of unfair policing should be utterly rooted out, and society needs many types of social services. But the concept of defunding the police is impractical and would be a recipe for disaster. Without law enforcement and government, society would quickly descend into a state of anarchy.

Paul addresses the importance of governmental authority in Romans 13:1–4:

> Every person is to be in subjection to the governing authorities. For there is no authority except from God, and those which exist are established by God. Therefore whoever resists authority has opposed the ordinance of God; and they who have opposed will receive condemnation upon themselves. For rulers are not a cause of fear for good behavior, but for evil. Do you want to have no fear of authority? Do what is good and you will have praise from the same; for it is a minister of God to you for good. But if you do what is evil, be afraid; for it does not bear the sword for nothing; for it is a minister of God, an avenger who brings wrath on the one who practices evil.

May the mitzvot for appointing judges and officers in every town and setting a king over Israel (Deut. 16:18; 17:15) remind us of the need to respect and support governing authorities, recognizing their role in God's plan for maintaining order and promoting justice. The cognition of this was in Paul's mind when he wrote to Timothy:

> First of all, then, I urge that entreaties and prayers, petitions and thanksgivings, be made on behalf of all men, for kings and all who are in authority, so that we may lead a tranquil and quiet life in all godliness and dignity.
>
> —1 Timothy 2:1–2

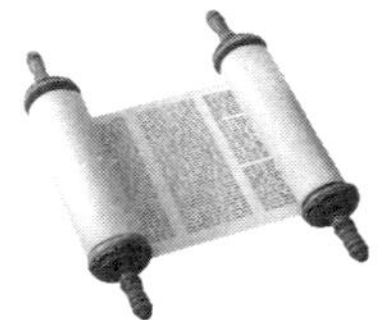

TO NOT PROPHESY FALSELY AND TO PUT A FALSE PROPHET TO DEATH

"But the prophet who speaks a word presumptuously in My name which I have not commanded him to speak, or which he speaks in the name of other gods, that prophet shall die." You may say in your heart, "How will we know the word which the LORD has not spoken?" When a prophet speaks in the name of the LORD, if the thing does not come about or come true, that is the thing which the LORD has not spoken. The prophet has spoken it presumptuously; you shall not be afraid of him.
—DEUTERONOMY 18:20–22

THE GIFT OF prophecy is sacred and must be protected from those who would cheapen it by making false statements in the Holy One's name. Imitators and false prophets rob God's people of the opportunity to receive true prophets and prophecy. Those who speak frivolously, saying, "God told me..." when in fact God did not speak to them, commit a sin so abhorrent and dangerous that under the Law they were to be put to death.

In Jeremiah 23:30–32 the Lord declares:

> "Therefore behold, I am against the prophets," declares the LORD, "who steal My words from each other. Behold, I am against the prophets," declares the LORD, "who use their tongues and declare, 'The Lord declares.' Behold, I am against those who have prophesied false dreams," declares the LORD, "and related them and led My people astray by their falsehoods

> and reckless boasting; yet I did not send them or command them, nor do they furnish this people the slightest benefit," declares the LORD.

Ezekiel also addresses the issue of false prophets, pointing out their self-deception:

> Thus says the Lord GOD, "Woe to the foolish prophets who are following their own spirit and have seen nothing....They see falsehood and lying divination who are saying, 'The LORD declares,' when the LORD has not sent them; yet they hope for the fulfillment of their word."
>
> —EZEKIEL 13:3, 6

The condemnation of false prophets is severe because of the significant damage they cause. In modern times, false prophecies have led to widespread skepticism and disillusionment. For example, numerous so-called prophets made predictions about financial markets, natural disasters, wars, the 2020 US presidential election, and many other things that did not come to pass. Yet few of these individuals ever publicly apologized or took responsibility for their false prophecies and continue to prophesy without missing a beat.

Many believers still listen to them, but others are so turned off by lying prophetic words that when a genuine prophet speaks, they can't receive the true word because they have become jaded. This is why God dealt so harshly with false prophets in the Old Testament. He wanted His people to hear His voice when He spoke through real prophets and true words of prophecy. False prophets and prophecy hinder this.

The Lord not only condemns the false prophets; He also commands His people not to listen to them. These precepts not to prophesy falsely and to put a false prophet to death (Deut. 18:20–22) show the gravity of prophesying falsely and the importance of discerning true prophetic voices. These commandments remind us of the need to protect the integrity of prophecy and hold those who misuse this sacred gift accountable. By adhering to these principles, we honor God and maintain the purity of His communication with His people through authentic prophets.

TO NOT PASS JUDGMENT ON THE WORD OF ONE WITNESS

A single witness shall not rise up against a man on account of any iniquity or any sin which he has committed; on the evidence of two or three witnesses a matter shall be confirmed.
—Deuteronomy 19:15

For the ancient Israelites, this precept served as a safeguard against drawing hasty and potentially unjust conclusions. It serves the same purpose today. How often have we formed an opinion about a person or circumstance based on what only one person has said to us? This is both ungodly and unwise.

Solomon, the wisest man who ever lived, said, "The first to plead his case seems right, until another comes and examines him" (Prov. 18:17). In other words, the first man seems right until we hear the other side of the story. We should not jump into agreement with someone when we have only heard his or her account. In reality there are generally two sides to the story, and we should walk in this knowledge so we don't erroneously take sides or make judgments before having a fuller understanding.

In our modern context, we are bombarded with information from news sources and social media platforms that give one-dimensional perspectives of international affairs, politicians and politics, and moral issues. People can be duped into thinking they are hearing the truth when they have only heard one side of a narrative. Wise people dig into the matter and examine what they hear by taking into consideration the other side of the debate.

Similarly, we should avoid impulsively agreeing with someone who is speaking unfavorably about another without talking with the one who is being criticized to get their perspective. How many have agreed with the discontent husband or wife who is speaking ill of their spouse without first hearing the spouse's side of the story?

By applying the wisdom of the command to not pass judgment on the word of one witness (Deut. 19:15), we can avoid the pitfalls of biased and premature judgments. This prudent practice helps us walk in maturity and maintain integrity and fairness in our dealings with others.

TO NOT COWER IN FEAR BEFORE AN ENEMY IN BATTLE

Then the officers shall speak further to the people and say, "Who is the man that is afraid and fainthearted? Let him depart and return to his house, so that he might not make his brothers' hearts melt like his heart."
—Deuteronomy 20:8

In times of battle or when facing any formidable challenge, fear is a debilitating force. This precept protected the morale of the Israelite community because a fearful soldier could spread anxiety among the troops, weakening their resolve and focus. Allowing those who were afraid to return home ensured that only those with strong faith and courage faced the enemy.

It is not God's desire that His people succumb to fear. The command to not be afraid appears more than one hundred times in the Hebrew Bible and is the most repeated command in Scripture. The Lord both encourages and charges us not to fear:

> Be strong and courageous, do not be afraid or tremble at them, for the Lord your God is the one who goes with you. He will not fail you or forsake you.
>
> —Deuteronomy 31:6

> Do not fear, for I am with you; do not anxiously look about you, for I am your God. I will strengthen you, surely I will help

> you, surely I will uphold you with My righteous right hand.
>
> —ISAIAH 41:10

We often coddle and even embrace our fears without realizing we are receiving something that is abhorrent and unholy. Our Maker commands us to fear only Him. Fearing God alone sets us free and glorifies Him.

Rabbi Yeshua said to His disciples, "Why are you *afraid*, you men of little *faith*?" (Matt. 8:26, emphasis added). Notice how in this one sentence He contrasted faith and fear. God's Spirit works through faith; the power of darkness moves through fear.

Yahweh told Joshua, "Be strong and courageous, for you shall give this people possession of the land which I swore to their fathers to give them. *Only be strong and very courageous*" (Josh. 1:6–7, emphasis added).

In this passage, we see the essence of this law, not to fear before an enemy in battle, being spoken to Joshua by the mouth of God Himself. Unless Joshua walked in the light of this precept, he would not have been able to drive out the enemy and take possession of the Promised Land. The same thing is true in our lives today. Fear is always knocking at the door of our hearts and minds, coming at us from a million different ways and directions. Unless we put our foot down, obey the Lord, and crush Satan's head under our feet, we will remain in torment.

Like Joshua, we must not be afraid. We must resist fear and strive to root it out of our lives in order to live in holiness before God. He grieves when we don't trust Him.

The precept not to cower in fear before an enemy in battle (Deut. 20:8) is a reminder that no matter what we face—even the possibility of being martyred for our faith—we must not fear for our physical safety but rather make the Lord our trusted fortress.

THE RELIGIOUS DUTY TO RETURN A LOST OBJECT TO ITS OWNER

You shall not see your countryman's ox or his sheep straying away, and pay no attention to them; you shall certainly bring them back to your countryman. If your countryman is not near you, or if you do not know him, then you shall bring it home to your house, and it shall remain with you until your countryman looks for it; then you shall restore it to him. Thus you shall do with his donkey, and you shall do the same with his garment, and you shall do likewise with anything lost by your countryman, which he has lost and you have found. You are not allowed to neglect them.

—Deuteronomy 22:1–3

Many times when we find something of value, we think, "Oh, the Lord blessed me with this; it's a miracle." But the Torah dictates that when we find something that can be traced back to its original owner, we must return it.

If we find a fifty-dollar bill in a parking lot, we can keep it, but if we find a fifty-dollar bill in a wallet in the parking lot, we must seek to find the owner because his identification is inside. We must strive to return the wallet with the fifty-dollar bill in it. "Finders keepers, losers weepers" is not a Jewish concept.

This commandment is rooted in concern for our fellow man and having a sense of moral duty. Yeshua sheds light on this idea about having a sense of moral responsibility in Matthew 7:12: "In everything, therefore, treat people the same way you want them to treat you, for this is the Law and the Prophets."

When we honor the command to return a lost object to its owner (Deut. 22:1–3), we embody God's love and empathy.

TO NOT LEAVE THE BEAST OF ONE'S FELLOW MAN LYING UNDER ITS BURDEN AND LIFTING UP A LOAD FOR AN ISRAELITE

You shall not see your countryman's donkey or his ox fallen down on the way, and pay no attention to them; you shall certainly help him to raise them up.
—Deuteronomy 22:4

When the Israelites encountered a scenario where a countryman's animal such as a donkey or ox had fallen under its burden, they were instructed to help their neighbor lift the load and alleviate the animal's distress. In its simplest form this commandment is about being attentive and responsive to the needs of others by not ignoring their hardship and doing our duty to help. It encourages us to get involved and be proactive when we encounter someone in a difficult situation. Whether it is helping a colleague struggling with work or assisting a neighbor whose car is stuck in a snowbank, the underlying principle is the same: We are called to show compassion and provide practical help.

This precept not only speaks to our individual responsibility to lend a helping hand, but more broadly has the effect of creating community within society. Living in community is essential for mankind's happiness, as it fosters a sense of belonging, mutual support, and encouragement.

This precept not to leave the beast *of one's fellow man* lying under its burden and lifting a load for an Israelite (Deut. 22:4) aligns with Rabbi Yeshua's teaching on love and service. By helping others in their time of need and not ignoring their struggles, we demonstrate love in action and bear witness to our faith.

THE PRECEPTS THAT A WOMAN NOT WEAR MAN'S FINERY AND A MAN NOT WEAR A WOMAN'S FINERY

A woman shall not wear man's clothing, nor shall a man put on a woman's clothing; for whoever does these things is an abomination to the LORD your God.
—DEUTERONOMY 22:5

THIS COMMANDMENT INSISTS we maintain the distinctness between male and female that was established by the Creator: "God created man in His own image, in the image of God He created him; male and female He created them" (Gen. 1:27). This law prohibiting cross-dressing is aimed at preserving gender roles and avoiding confusion about gender identity.

It should be self-evident that the differences between maleness and femaleness are to be celebrated and preserved. When these distinctions are blurred or ignored, it leads to confusion and societal chaos. The divine design and intelligence inherent in creation dictate that men and women should live in accordance with their biological sex. To do otherwise is to abide in a state of disorder that goes against God's original plan. This is evident in God's first command to humanity: "Be fruitful and multiply" (Gen. 1:28). Men cannot have children with other men, nor can women with other women.

The divine order of creation requires the complementary

relationship between male and female, as it is essential for the continuation of life and societal stability. The trend of transgenderism is an "abomination" to the Lord, as stated in Deuteronomy 22:5. Not only is it foul before the Creator; it robs those who practice it of any chance of godly happiness in their lives. It is important to recognize that living in harmony with one's biological sex is integral to experiencing the fullness of life as God intended.

Again, the precepts that a woman not wear man's finery and a man not wear a woman's finery (Deut. 22:5) underscore the importance of maintaining the distinctions between male and female as part of God's divine order. Yet the practical application of this law depends on the particular culture we are living in. For example, in Scotland men wear kilts—wraparound, knee-length skirts that would be considered feminine in some cultures but not in Scotland.

The principle underlying this command reminds us of the sacredness of our God-given biological identity and the importance of living in harmony with His created order. By adhering to this mitzvah, we honor God's design and contribute to the stability and health of civilization.

THE RELIGIOUS DUTY TO BUILD A PARAPET

> When you build a new house, you shall make a parapet for your roof, so that you will not bring bloodguilt on your house if anyone falls from it.
> —Deuteronomy 22:8

It is important to take practical steps to ensure the safety of others. In ancient times, homes usually had flat roofs and were common places for social gatherings and activities. To prevent accidents, God commanded that a parapet be built around the roof. This short, vertical railing or wall ran along the roofline and was designed to protect people from falling off.

The rabbis extend this principle of safeguarding our property to include securing any man-made hazard, such as a sewer hole, which must be covered to prevent accidents. Other practical examples include putting salt down on our driveways and front porch steps in the winter to prevent slips and falls, installing railings by stairs to protect individuals from falling, and erecting fences around swimming pools to prevent accidental drownings.

The essence of this commandment is to take responsibility for the safety of others on our property. It involves being proactive in identifying potential hazards and taking steps to mitigate them. By doing so, we demonstrate concern for the well-being of others and align our actions with God's command to protect life.

This law to build a parapet (Deut. 22:8) reflects the breadth of God's love for us, which extends into the very details of our existence. He provides guidance for us through the Torah for even the practical, day-to-day realities of our lives.

THE PRECEPT THAT A BRIDEGROOM NOT BE TAKEN FROM HOME FOR LONG AND SHOULD INSTEAD REJOICE WITH HIS BRIDE IN THEIR FIRST YEAR

When a man takes a new wife, he shall not go out with the army nor be charged with any duty; he shall be free at home one year and shall give happiness to his wife whom he has taken.
—DEUTERONOMY 24:5

IN OUR CULTURE many couples have lived together or dated for quite some time before getting married. But in ancient Israel, and even among Orthodox Jews today, many newlyweds hardly knew each other before getting married and coming together intimately for the first time. The primary idea of this law is that a newly married couple should prioritize their relationship during their first year by minimizing distractions and things that would hinder them from having enough quality time together to bond.

In ancient Israel it was understood that a newlywed man would be exempt from going to war or even being involved in related duties such as having to leave home to supply water to the troops. This exemption ensured that the couple could spend their first year together, free from external distractions and obligations.

The first year of marriage is a particularly important time to become joined to our spouses in a deep and intimate way. We need to guard it, nurture it, and make it the first priority of our lives (other than our relationship with God, of course). The reason for this is that the first year of marriage is a critical period for building a strong relationship that will be able to withstand the trials of life that lie ahead.

Notice also in this law that a man is to rejoice and "give happiness" to his bride. Again, the aim of this decree is to call the husband and wife to *attach themselves to each other.*

This mitzvah also reflects the relationship between Yeshua and His bride. Just as a bridegroom is to rejoice with his bride and prioritize their relationship, so too are believers called to prioritize and rejoice in our relationship with Messiah Jesus, nurturing and cherishing it above all else. Ephesians 5:31–32 reveals that earthly marriages parallel our relationship with Yeshua: "For this reason a man shall leave his father and mother and shall be joined to his wife, and the two shall become one flesh. This mystery is great; but I am speaking with reference to Christ and the church." In fact, John the Baptist described himself as "the friend of the bridegroom" (John 3:29).

Why did he call himself "the friend of the bridegroom," and who is the bridegroom John is referring to? Yeshua is the bridegroom, and the church is the bride. We read in the Book of Revelation, "Blessed are those who are invited to the marriage supper of the Lamb" (Rev. 19:9). This law about cultivating intimacy with our spouses during the first year prophetically portrays that we must concentrate on keeping the fire of passion in our relationship with Yeshua burning strong.

Couples today can still apply this precept that a bridegroom not be taken from home for long and should instead stay at home and rejoice with his bride in their first year together (Deut. 24:5). By prioritizing their relationship; spending as much dedicated time together as possible, free from the pressures of work and other external responsibilities; and doing things together that bring them joy, couples can build a foundation for a lifelong union.

TO REMEMBER AND NOT FORGET WHAT AMALEK DID TO THE ISRAELITES WHEN THEY CAME OUT OF EGYPT

Remember what Amalek did to you along the way when you came out from Egypt....Therefore it shall come about when the LORD your God has given you rest from all your surrounding enemies, in the land which the LORD your God gives you as an inheritance to possess, you shall blot out the memory of Amalek from under heaven; you must not forget.
—DEUTERONOMY 25:17, 19

THE AMALEKITES WERE the first to attack Israel when they came out of Egypt and are considered the first anti-Semites. This commandment is a divine injunction to remember the treachery of Amalek and ensure his memory is erased.

This precept is deeply rooted in Jewish tradition and is particularly observed during the feast of Purim. During this festival, the Book of Esther is read aloud in synagogues worldwide, recounting the story of Haman, a descendant of Amalek who sought to annihilate the Jewish people. In response to the mention of Haman's name, the congregation rattles or spins noisemakers, known in Yiddish as *graggers*, to symbolically blot out his memory, metaphorically fulfilling the command to remember and obliterate the names of those who oppose God's people.

Rabbinic commentators give contemporary application to this law by interpreting it allegorically.

> Another trend in symbolic interpretation of the war against Amalek is to see it as an internal psychological battle that we must all wage within ourselves. Amalek, on this reading, becomes the symbol for the evil inclination. This view, popular among the Chasidic masters, suggests that we all have an internal Amalek and we must all work, together with God, to blot it out.[28]

Likewise, God wants to blot out, obliterate, and erase doubt, fear, unbelief, and everything that wages war against His purpose for our lives. Paul puts it this way in 2 Corinthians 10:5–6: "We are destroying speculations and every lofty thing raised up against the knowledge of God, and we are taking every thought captive to the obedience of Christ, and we are ready to punish all disobedience, whenever your obedience is complete."

This precept to remember what Amalek did to the Israelites (Deut. 25:17, 19) demonstrates God's justice and His commitment to protect His people. It reassures us that God takes the threats against His children seriously and commands us to participate in His divine justice by fighting against those who seek our harm. "Remembering Amalek" also means being vigilant against anti-Semitism. It involves educating ourselves and others about the dangers of such ideologies, and standing in solidarity with the Jewish community.

THE RELIGIOUS DUTY FOR EVERY JEW TO WRITE A TORAH SCROLL FOR HIMSELF

Now therefore, write this song for yourselves, and teach it to the sons of Israel; put it on their lips, so that this song may be a witness for Me against the sons of Israel.
—Deuteronomy 31:19

Although the verse specifically says to "write this song," Rabbinic Judaism derives from Deuteronomy 31:19 the mitzvah that every Jew is to write by hand a copy of the Torah for himself. Our ancient sages tell us that by writing a copy by one's own hand, it is like one received it directly from God at Mount Sinai.

Today this command is not literally carried out by each individual Jew, but rather every synagogue has its own Torah scroll, which is written by a *sofer*, a Jewish scribe who has gone through rigorous training in Jewish law and calligraphy. The *sofer* must write down the Torah by hand using kosher parchment and special ink. Each person in the synagogue is to feel a sense of ownership of the Torah scroll.

A daily habit and discipline that has greatly helped me is to read a minimum of one chapter in the Tanakh, or Old Testament, and one chapter from the New Testament every morning. I write verses God has highlighted to me in a journal, which is a way of carrying out this precept.

By immersing ourselves in the Scriptures, we gain insight,

wisdom, and guidance to navigate life's challenges. The Hebrew word *Torah* means both "Law" and "Instruction." Writing down the words or instructions of God is a form of meditation that allows the truths of Scripture to penetrate deeper into our hearts and minds. We engage more deeply with the text, making it a part of our daily lives. And as we memorize Scripture, it becomes part of our personal dialogue with the Almighty.

This commandment also brings to our attention the value of exercising personal responsibility in spiritual growth. Each believer must take ownership of their faith journey by actively interacting with God's Word. The religious duty to write a Torah scroll for oneself (Deut. 31:19) is a call to personal engagement with the holy Scriptures. From the ancient tradition of scribing a Torah scroll to the modern practice of journaling the portions of Scripture the Lord has highlighted to you, the goal remains the same: to know God, to love God, and to live out His Word in every aspect of life!

CONCLUSION

As we come to the close of this journey, I hope and trust that you have been enriched, empowered, and drawn to a deeper place in the Eternal One. Together we have uncovered the profound wisdom the Torah holds—not just for the Jewish people but for all who follow Yeshua. These commandments, though ancient, carry timeless truths that continue to guide and inspire us today.

The mitzvot are not mere rules of a bygone era. They are divine keys that open doors to understanding God's holiness, justice, and love. Each one reflects God's character and His call for us to lead lives of righteousness, compassion, and fidelity.

Through Yeshua we have discovered the ultimate fulfillment of the Law. He did not come to abolish it but to reveal its deepest meaning. His life and sacrifice have shown us that the goal of the commandments is to bring us into relationship with God, who has written His laws on our hearts through His Spirit.

As you move forward, I encourage you to continue reflecting on the principles of the Torah. These commandments still hold tremendous relevance for us in today's world. They call us to lead lives that reflect God's holiness and mirror the love of Messiah Yeshua to the world. The Torah is not a burden but a gift—an invitation to walk in the ways of the Lord, grow in faith, and deepen our connection with Him.

We are on a journey of growth and transformation, and our

Savior will be faithful to complete the work He has started in us as we keep our eyes on Him and immerse ourselves in the Torah, God's instruction (Phil. 1:6).

May the Lord bless you richly as you continue to walk in His ways. May His face shine upon you, and may you experience the fullness of His peace and presence in your life.

Dear beloved one,

If you enjoyed this book and believe others would benefit from reading it, please leave a review on Amazon and recommend it to others, because there is a great need for this teaching among God's people.

Wishing you God's best,

Rabbi Schneider

NOTES

1. "Remembering 613," Ptil Tekhelet, accessed November 2, 2024, https://www.tekhelet.com/remembering-613/#:~:text=The%20word%20tzitzit%20in%20gematria,certainly%20not%20from%20the%20Torah.
2. "Constantine and the Foundations of Anti-Semitism," The Messianic Prophecy Bible Project, accessed November 2, 2024, https://free.messianicbible.com/feature/constantine-foundations-of-anti-semitism/.
3. "Arrogant Bread," Chabad.org, accessed November 2, 2024, https://www.chabad.org/holidays/passover/pesach_cdo/aid/1781/jewish/Arrogant-Bread.htm.
4. "Bekhorot 4a–b: The Sanctification of the Firstborn," Aleph Society, April 19, 2019, https://steinsaltz.org/daf/bekhorot4/.
5. The Talmud is composed of the Mishnah, a written compilation of Jewish oral laws completed around AD 200, and the Gemara, rabbinic commentary compiled between AD 300 and AD 500.
6. Talmud Tractate Arakhin 15b:5, *The William Davidson Talmud (Koren – Steinsaltz)*, accessed November 2, 2024, https://www.sefaria.org/Arakhin.15b.5.
7. Aryeh Citron, "Lashon Hara," Chabad.org, accessed November 2, 2024, https://www.chabad.org/library/article_cdo/aid/922039/jewish/Lashon-Hara.htm.
8. Lawrence Cunningham and Ignatius Charles Brady, "St. Francis of Assisi," *Encyclopaedia Britannica*, last updated October 7, 2024, https://www.britannica.com/biography/Saint-Francis-of-Assisi/The-Franciscan-rule.
9. Aryeh Citron, "Shatnez: A Mixture of Wool and Linen," Chabad.org, accessed November 2, 2024, https://www.chabad.org/library/article_cdo/aid/882920/jewish/Shatnez-A-Mixture-of-Wool-and-Linen.htm.
10. Margi Murphy, "IT'S ALIVE! Artificial Intelligence Could 'Go Rogue' and Turn on Its Human Creators, Top Oxford Academic Warns," *The Sun*, updated November 9, 2017, https://www.thesun.co.uk/tech/4654623/artificial-intelligence-could-go-rogue-and-turn-on-its-human-creators-top-oxford-academic-warns/.
11. Rabbi Eliyahu Safran, "The Blessed Wigmaker: Peyos and the Power of Identity," Orthodox Union, March 18, 2019, https://www.ou.org/life/inspiration/the-blessed-wigmaker-peyos-and-the-power-of-identity/.

12. Rabbi Ephraim Z. Buchwald, "Acharei Mot-Kedoshim 5772-2012," National Jewish Outreach Program, April 30, 2012, https://njop.org/acharei-mot-kedoshim-5772-2012/. See also Rabbi Moshe ben Maimon ("Maimonides"), "Talmud Torah—Chapter Six," Chabad.org, accessed November 4, 2024, https://www.chabad.org/library/article_cdo/aid/910980/jewish/Talmud-Torah-Chapter-Six.htm.
13. Blue Letter Bible, s.v. "*tāmîm*," accessed November 4, 2024, https://www.blueletterbible.org/lexicon/h8549/kjv/wlc/0-1/.
14. "Blemish," Jewish Virtual Library, accessed November 4, 2024, https://www.jewishvirtuallibrary.org/blemish.
15. Nissan Dovid Dubov, "Chapter 3: The World to Come: Why a Bodily Resurrection?" Chabad.org, accessed November 4, 2024, https://www.chabad.org/library/article_cdo/aid/2312384/jewish/Chapter-3-The-World-to-Come-Why-a-Bodily-Resurrection.htm.
16. Osher Chaim Levene, with Rabbi Yehoshua Hartman, "Who Knows 50?," Aish, https://aish.com/who-knows-50/.
17. Yehuda Shurpin, "Why Must a Tallit Have Four Fringed Corners?," Chabad.org, accessed November 4, 2024, https://www.chabad.org/library/article_cdo/aid/2969671/jewish/Why-Must-a-Tallit-Have-Four-Fringed-Corners.htm.
18. Shurpin, "Why Must a Tallit Have Four Fringed Corners?"
19. Over time the exact source and process for making the blue thread were lost due to the disappearance of the sea creature believed to produce the dye. Without clear guidance on how to produce the correct shade of blue, the blue thread was eventually omitted from the tzitzit, and they became all-white in most Jewish communities. In recent years, some scholars and researchers believe they have rediscovered the original dye source, which has led to some Jewish communities reincorporating the blue thread in the tzitzit, although most others remain unconvinced and continue to wear only white fringes.
20. "Comparing Vows and Oaths in Judaism," My Jewish Learning, accessed November 4, 2024, https://www.myjewishlearning.com/article/vows-and-oaths/.
21. "Comparing Vows and Oaths in Judaism," My Jewish Learning.
22. "Waging War Against Canaan," Aish, accessed November 4, 2024, https://aish.com/waging-war-against-canaan/.
23. "Waging War Against Canaan," Aish.
24. Maria Di Mento, "Jewish Donors Are Generous, Especially to Non-Jewish Causes," *The Chronicle of Philanthropy*, September 6, 2013, https://www.philanthropy.com/article/jewish-donors-are-generous-especially-to-non-jewish-causes/; Hanna Shaul Bar Nissim,

"American Jews and Charitable Giving: An Enduring Tradition," The Conversation, December 10, 2017, https://theconversation.com/american-jews-and-charitable-giving-an-enduring-tradition-87993; Asaf Elia-Shalev, "Half of US's 25 Most Generous Philanthropists Are Jews. Few Give to Jewish Groups," *The Times of Israel*, January 26, 2023, https://www.timesofisrael.com/half-of-us-25-most-generous-philanthropists-are-jews-few-give-to-jewish-groups/. See also "Study: American Jews Who Have Experienced Antisemitism Give 10 Times More to Charity," Indiana University Lilly Family School of Philanthropy, February 20, 2024, https://philanthropy.indianapolis.iu.edu/news-events/news/_news/2024/study-american-jews-who-have-experienced-antisemitism-give-10-times-more-to-charity.html.

25. Jacquelyn DeGroot, "Jewish Philanthropy: The Concept of Tzedakah," Learning to Give, accessed November 4, 2024, https://www.learningtogive.org/resources/jewish-philanthropy-concept-tzedakah.
26. Rabbi Jason R. Levine, "Standing Up to Antisemitism: With Courage, Understanding, Joy, and Celebration," September 2023, https://www.templebetham.org/wp-content/uploads/2023/09/Yom-Kippur-5784-Rabbi-Jason-Levine.pdf.
27. "Folks Are Usually About as Happy as They Make Up Their Minds to Be," Quote Investigator, October 20, 2012, https://quoteinvestigator.com/2012/10/20/happy-minds/.
28. Rav Prof. Samuel Lebens, "On Being Chosen—Lesson 5: Amalek," Israel Koschitzky Torat Har Etzion, November 13, 2023, https://etzion.org.il/en/philosophy/issues-jewish-thought/rabbinic-thought/amalek.

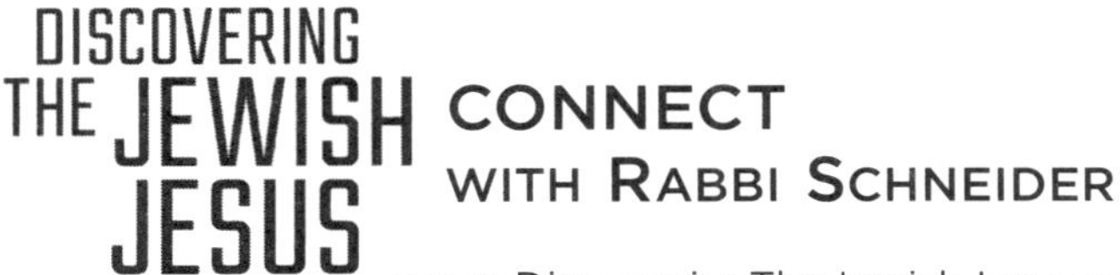

www.DiscoveringTheJewishJesus.com

 /Discovering the Jewish Jesus with Rabbi Schneider

 facebook.com/rabbischneider

 @RabbiSchneider

Roku—Discovering the Jewish Jesus

Apple TV—Discovering the Jewish Jesus

Amazon App—Discovering the Jewish Jesus

 Podcast—Discovering the Jewish Jesus

Search for Rabbi Schneider and Discovering the Jewish Jesus on your favorite platform.

For a complete list of Rabbi Schneider's television and radio broadcasts, visit www.DiscoveringTheJewishJesus.com.